Bolaño

Bolaño

• • •

A BIOGRAPHY
in CONVERSATIONS

• • •

Mónica Maristain

Translated by Kit Maude

MELVILLE HOUSE
BROOKLYN

BOLAÑO

First Melville House Printing: September 2014

Melville House Publishing
145 Plymouth Street
Brooklyn, NY 11201

mhpbooks.com   facebook.com/mhpbooks   @melvillehouse

Library of Congress Control Number: 2014946863

ISBN: 978-1-61219-347-2

Manufactured in the United States of America
1 3 5 7 9 10 8 6 4 2

Contents

Acknowledgments

Thanks to Martín Solares, for your confidence; Guillermo Quijas, for your trust and patience; Ricardo House, for the interviews and collaboration; Melina Maristain, for the transcripts and love; and Alejandro Páez Varela.

Grateful acknowledgment is made to Ricardo House for the permission to quote from interviews from his film *Roberto Bolaño, la batalla futura* (The Future Battle), a documentary in three parts, made with Ignacio Echevarría. The chapter "Mr. Beach's Son" was written in collaboration with the contemporary Argentine poet Diana Bellessi.

A Note

A complete biography of Roberto Bolaño will not be possible without access to the writer's correspondence, diaries, and unpublished work. This work is thus provisional: it relies on conversations with Bolaño's parents, friends, and colleagues, as well as members of his Infrarealist literary movement in Mexico and his literary circle in Spain. I have also interviewed a group of literary writers and critics who have been influenced by Bolaño's work. These new dialogues are presented alongside newspaper and television interviews—with the aim of providing a portrait of Bolaño that goes beyond what we can see of the author in his novels, poems, and essays.

Introduction

Whenever I think of Roberto Bolaño, I remember a poem that I know by heart: "Definitions with Which to Await My Death," by the great Argentine lyricist and poet Homero Manzi:

> I know that my name will resound in the ears of
>   my loved ones
> as perfectly as a picture.
> And I also know that sometimes it will cease to
>   be a name
> and will just be a pair of meaningless words.

The poem strikes a special chord with me because, even though years have passed since the insurmountable loss of Roberto Bolaño, a decade is just a drop in the infinite ocean of time, and he remains perfectly preserved in the memories of the people who knew him.

It's not very likely that the author who changed the face of literature in Latin America will ever become "a pair of meaningless words," but this verse placed next to a person whose shadow actually grows with the passage of time takes on new power if you consider that the author of *The Savage Detectives* expressed a lot of contradictory, and some might say *meaningless*, things about himself. He remains to those who didn't know him, and some who did, a mystery.

I first came in contact with Roberto Bolaño to request an interview. Though sick with liver disease, he quickly agreed to a conversation; he said he was still breathing and would be happy to do an interview, especially one that was relaxed, frivolous, and "almost" posthumous. These were the sorts of conversations, he wrote, that he liked best.

The interview ended up being his last, and it caused a commotion when it was published. This wasn't the result of the journalist's skill but the power of the subject and the fact that it was published the month that he died, July 2003, in *Playboy México*. At the time it wasn't easy to get a long interview with Bolaño published in a Mexican magazine, but that month's edition had a strong cover, with a very famous cover model, and the editor wrote: "We've got some leeway here; let's rescue that interview with Bolaño—the issue will sell lots of copies anyway."

Bolaño was not a casual interview subject. I don't quite know how it came about, but there was a long period during my work on the interview in which I would get e-mails from "robertoba," his e-mail name, and they would always be the bearers of happiness and joy. They would tell me to take care of my mother, to say hello to my sister, not to drink or smoke, and to publish, if possible, a story by Rodrigo Fresán, an Argentine fiction writer now living in Spain, in the magazine. They would wish me luck with the play I was producing, but warn me that I shouldn't even think about quitting *Playboy*.

One day he wrote to me at a quarter past three in the morning, his time, telling me about a long night spent caring for his two-year-old daughter, and how he had eventually put her to sleep by turning on *La Dolce Vita*. He had recently traveled to Italy and discovered that life there sometimes felt like a Fellini

movie, which, he thought, wasn't all that surprising: having dinner in an old Italian quarter was bound to bring Fellini to mind.
He was at this point waiting for a liver transplant—he said he
was third in line—and was passing the time in part by reading
German crime novels. By the third page, he wrote, he could figure
out who the murderer was, and by the tenth he had the feeling the
detective was a real idiot. He wasn't shy in our correspondence:
"Please keep writing," he requested.

On other occasions we argued: about Lula, who had been
elected president of Brazil in 2002; about Mexico; about Argentine and Chilean wines—he erroneously believed that the latter
were superior. And he always ended conversations with an irre-
sistibly sweet phrase.

•   •   •

I found out that Bolaño had died when a friend called me very
early from Spain. "Moni, have you heard?" said my friend.

My brief correspondence had given me a glimpse of an amaz-
ingly generous writer. Afterward, I started to ask myself how the
people who knew him best remembered the great author. The
ones who had enjoyed many long conversations with him. The
ones with whom he had shared his youth, childhood, and
maturity. This was the motivation for writing this book: to find
out more about Bolaño, from the people who played important
roles in his life.

My project here has been to make some attempt to bring him
back, to let those who knew him best have their say. It was impossible to include all of them. That wasn't the intention. Many of the
voices presented here, however, confirm what we already knew
to some extent from Bolaño's fiction: he was an extraordinary
individual. The Chilean political activist Rodrigo Quijada, now

also deceased, is quoted in these pages as saying, "Bolaño is one of those people you meet at a certain moment in your life who you will always remember clearly and with great fondness. People who have met Bolaño know that what I'm saying is true. He is the kind of man you miss at a gathering. 'If only Bolaño were here,' we used to say when someone started to get unbearable."[1] The book aspires to this spirit.

Bolaño

1

When His Father
Bought Him a Horse

*The taste of pebre salsa and charquicán—Quilpué
was very pretty*

In the 1950s, Santiago de Chile was freezing cold. The houses didn't have central heating, and the beautiful trees that now add a touch of green to the Chilean capital had not yet been planted. The world was experiencing profound social and political change, but in Santiago time seemed to be standing still. Men wore sober suits and ties and acted with a formality that Chilean society took years to shake off. Santiago was a gray city.

Into this setting of concrete and mist, Roberto Bolaño was born, on April 28, 1953. The son of truck driver and professional boxer León Bolaño and primary school teacher Victoria Ávalos, he was delivered in a Seguro Social clinic a few blocks away from Recoleta Avenue, where his paternal grandparents lived.

Victoria and León's firstborn child didn't spend a long time in the city. Soon after his birth, the family moved to Valparaíso, about seventy miles from Santiago. Valparaíso is a major city, Chile's third-largest, and a thriving seaport. As Bolaño later recalled, he was born in Santiago but never lived in Santiago.[1] In Valparaíso the family lived on Los Placeres hill, but they were soon on the move again. They moved to Quilpué, into a country house, and later still to Viña and Cauquenes, nearby areas populated by alcoholics and spiritualists, according to Bolaño.

Years later, Bolaño would chiefly recall the food in Chile, including a pepper plantation that was cultivated by a worker hired by his father on a small plot of land in Quilpué.

BOLAÑO: The hellish part in Chile was my childhood and adolescence. And then the coup d'état. But I like Chilean food. Have you ever tried it? It's pretty good cuisine. Empanadas, corn tart, humitas, Chilean stew, seafood, perhaps the best I've ever had, that sauce they call pebre, which may be simple but is nonetheless very effective, charquicán, which is a dish that dates back to before the War of Independence and they say was Manuel Rodríguez's favorite.[2]

Manuel Rodríguez, who was assassinated in 1818, was one of the founders of an independent Chile. It was in Quilpué that Roberto, at seven years of age, had a horse he named Poncho Roto—Broken Poncho—which he memorializes in his story "Last Evenings on Earth."

The story describes a trip that a father and son make to Acapulco. His father, León Bolaño, remembers it thus: "We were both alone at home, so we got into the car and left. Roberto never liked driving. The car in the story was a Dodge, then I bought a Mercedes and I gave him the keys to the Dodge but he didn't want it. He said to me: 'Papa, take the keys, people are dying of hunger in India and you want to give me a car …'"[3]

Bolaño's childhood in Chile was idyllic, despite some later protestations to the contrary. These were the early years of his parents' marriage, which would later disintegrate. But the family was close at the time. On the weekends Victoria Ávalos's father would come to eat chicken cooked in the clay oven León had built at the country house in Quilpué. "It was all very pretty, very pretty," León remembers.[4]

2

Mama's Asthma

Bolaño's pregnant silence—Father the sportsman—Cultured, not simple—A song by the Who

The Bolaño family moved to Mexico in 1968, when Roberto was fifteen. The reason was Victoria's poor health: she suffered from chronic asthma. According to Bolaño's father:

LEÓN BOLAÑO: They started to treat her [in Mexico] on the recommendation of a Mexican doctor. I stayed with the two children in Chile, sent her off for a few months and she came back well. That's how it was for me: I was screwed. I had to pay for the trip and the hotel and the doctor. But in the end, it didn't do any good because the year she came back the bronchitis flared up again. A doctor who was a friend of mine told me that if she always recovered in Mexico, we should go to live there or my children would end up without a mother. I sold everything I had in Chile, and we went to live in Mexico City. Roberto was fifteen at the time. The four of us lived together for a few years until my wife and I separated. I kept Roberto, and she went to Spain with our daughter.[1]

The family spent the first few months in Mexico at the home of some friends of Victoria's who had come to study in Mexico City. Then they rented a house in the Nápoles neighborhood, which León, who was looking for work at the time, found "very expensive." Eventually they settled at Calle Samuel 27 in the Guadalupe Tepeyac neighborhood, in a three-story building that had been loaned to them.

As a teenager, Bolaño was a borderline agoraphobic, and he spent his first years in Mexico stuck at home, moving between the bedroom and the living room, smoking and writing, according to his friend, the poet Jaime Quezada, who lived in the house for a year at the invitation of Bolaño's mother.

After Roberto died, Quezada wrote a book called *Bolaño antes de Bolaño* (Bolaño Before Bolaño) in which, among other anecdotes, he succinctly but evocatively describes the teenager who lived on Calle Samuel:

> QUEZADA: At that time he was an eighteen-, nineteen-year-old boy, he had come to Mexico with his parents when he was very young, several years before the military coup of '73. By now, he had basically left secondary school and spent his days and nights reading and rereading (Kafka, Eliot, Proust, Joyce, Borges, Paz, Cortázar, García Márquez), and smoking and smoking and drinking big mugs of milky tea, always angry with himself or someone else, an anger that didn't sit well on his pale, smooth face or precocious intellectual gaze ... Roberto was something of a Kaspar Hauser ... who never left the bedroom/living room/dining room except to go to the bathroom or to declaim something loudly, pulling on his thick head of hair, about a passage in the book he was reading. Or to accompany me patiently—he was such a patient and impatient reader—to the soda fountain on the corner, where I drank a beer and he had a guava smoothie.[2]

Guadalupe Tepeyac is, and was in the 1970s, very much a workers' neighborhood, with its taco and tamale stalls on the sidewalks, and its street markets. The Mexican capital at the time was exploding with the bloody student protests of 1968, and the Olympic Games were being held there. Though bookish, Bolaño, on moving to the big city, would have surely seen its seedier undercurrents. He would have walked Calzadas Guadalupe and De los Misterios, which generously offered shelter to giant urban rodents, the flamboyant devotees of the Virgin of Guadalupe, and a motley community that lent color and life to the long pedestrian stretch that runs from Eje 2, a major road, to the Basilica of Guadalupe.

But the events of 1968 were not far from Bolaño's view either: The Olympic flame burned just a few blocks away from the Bolaño family's home. The Tlatelolco massacre of students on October 2, when dozens and maybe hundreds were killed on the eve of the Olympics, occurred very close to them as well. Not even Roberto, with his libertine dedication to becoming a tobacco-addled ghost wandering his house in search of the perfect phrase, would have been unmoved by the social upheaval the country was experiencing at the time. In fact, what better than that oppressive, heaving atmosphere for the gestation of his novel *Amulet*, an exhilarating account of the life of the Uruguayan woman Auxilio Lacouture, who locked herself in the Universidad Nacional Autónoma de México (UNAM) bathroom during the military occupation of the university?

Things might have been very different for the foreign son of working-class parents in the snobbish environs of the La Condesa, Coyoacán, or Polanco neighborhoods, which were and still are white, upper-middle-class areas whose inhabitants, although many undoubtedly very progressive, are, in the excellent phrase of Junot Díaz, "more interested in calling each other *fresas* [snobs/posh/superficial] than really making themselves a part of the city where they live." The segregation by class might have made it seem impossible, during this period, for a Mexican from La Condesa, Coyoacán, or Polanco to visit a home in Guadalupe Tepeyac, where Bolaño lived.

The writer Carmen Boullosa, an icon of sophisticated Mexico City, described Bolaño's sense of otherness in the posh capital: "The first image of Bolaño that comes into my head is that of a curious young man, the only one wearing ironed clothes because all the others were shabby, filthy poets, with rubber sandals and a kind of scruffy, post-hippie look.[3] Bolaño was wearing ironed clothes, and had long hair. He had that rebelliousness which was so much a part of him, but he was also very preppy." When Roberto Bolaño's social background is discussed, his working-class family is rarely mentioned. In Latin America, working class isn't the same thing as poor: they're very different concepts. The ironed clothes mentioned by Boullosa are a stamp of distinction that every working family puts stock in: to be dressed neatly is to assume the aristocratic trappings of someone who comes from a home determined to "go places." Such tidiness was less important in the nicer neighborhoods of Mexico City during the late 1960s.

León Bolaño, his father, worked hard at various jobs his whole life to put a roof over his children's heads and food on their table. And Roberto, in fact, was economically dependent on his father until he was past twenty years old. A silence lasting nearly two decades came between them after the son asked his father, from Europe, for "a few dollars as an advance on my inheritance."

"That upset me a lot, an advance on what inheritance? I hadn't died yet," said an elderly León Bolaño. The subject clearly still rankled with him.[4]

Free of the vicissitudes of a middle class that in Latin America usually decides the political fate of its countries, Roberto was a spoiled child and a teenager who wasn't subject to the usual social mores. As is common in aristocratic families, or those with a historic upper-class pedigree, many lower-class families were at the time happy for their children to possess essential moral values while being much more lax about conforming to more superficial social norms. These families didn't care about what people might say. This is where lower-class families coincide with the upper-class: they both provide a liberal environment for their children's upbringing and encourage them to seek out their own destiny at a very early age. This was the case with Roberto.

He found his destiny in books, and he devoted himself to it with the dedication of a saint. It might sound romantic, but that doesn't make it any less true. As can be seen throughout his work, Bolaño drew on his prodigious ability to create authentic worlds from fiction. Who else but the Chilean writer could portray the essence of the north of Mexico without ever having been to Ciudad Juárez or Tijuana? Bolaño was able to strip away the veils of contemporary Mexico one by one even though he lived there for only seven years and never returned. He gleaned his method and meaning from the books he devoured ravenously in his childhood, and it was books Bolaño referenced when he thought of himself as a literary hero, the inhabitant of a fictional territory that he loved to enter as a hero and, often, leave as a victim.

From his father's memory: "Books were all he cared about. At night he would leave his room to go to the dining room and tap away at the typewriter. Then he'd wander around for a bit before going back to the typewriter and smoking. He smoked so much!"

An anecdote from Jaime Quezada provides a vivid image of a teenager dedicated to storytelling. He had a flaw common to young writers: self-pity, the need to look oneself in the mirror and see a misunderstood soul, too much of a visionary for the blank faces and narrow minds of the real world.

QUEZADA: When he was eighteen, Roberto thought that he was a character from a rock song and said to his friend: "It's as though that song were written about me ..." It's about a boy who can barely sleep at night and at one point he says to his father: "Father, I can't sleep." The father remembers an old photograph he has in his desk. He looks for the picture and hands it to him. The photograph is a pornographic image of a naked woman. The boy looks at the lurid photo several times. He gets turned on and masturbates. And then he goes to sleep happily, without any trouble. The next day he says to his father: "Introduce me to the girl in the photograph." And the father answers: "But she died forty years ago!" And that's how the rock story ends. It's a great, genuine story for a song!

Bolaño was talking about the song "Pictures of Lily" by the Who. Roberto, who compared his life with that of the ordinary boy in the lyrics of a rock song, continued to see himself throughout his life as a literary character, a fictional person. Proof of this comes from the letters he wrote to his friends, which Bolaño's first publisher, the American Juan Pascoe, describes as "Literary acts, not personal letters. He was not really writing … He was writing what he wanted to write at that moment. He was writing for an audience, creating a document for posterity."[5]

3

Mr. Beach's Son

You might say that I'm not particularly elegant—"That woman"—I have to educate my children or I'll go crazy—Roberto had a lot of balls—My father's truck broken down on a desert road—Papa, I'm thirsty—Roberto was never a drug addict!—Drinking coffee, writing, and exchanging ideas—The pen moved before he could come up with the phrases

León Bolaño was born in Bio Bio, Los Ángeles, Chile, in 1927. His parents were Spanish—Catalan, to be precise—and came over on a ship that docked at the Chilean port of Talcahuano. He became a truck driver and a boxer and his physique won him many a strongman competition, which were often held on the beaches of Chile.

So León Bolaño is Mr. Beach. At eighty-three years old, when he agreed to speak for this profile, he still preserved a certain presence and strapping, upright body, virtues that his son didn't much care for. León Bolaño died in December 2010, at age eighty-four. His parents had nine children, but only two were alive when we spoke: "All the others died of massive heart attacks," he says.

The writer Juan Villoro says that the day after León and Roberto met in Barcelona, after more than two decades without seeing each other, Roberto said to his son: "I give you my full permission to shoot me if I'm like my father when I'm old." Roberto was annoyed by the fact that León was a man who didn't read books, that he—perhaps—didn't have the sensitivity that was so prevalent in his mother, the teacher Victoria Ávalos, who, according to Bolaño's editor Jorge Herralde, "was the great mentor to Roberto's literary career."

Bolaño's assessment was: "No, you might say that I'm not particularly elegant. I'm the grandson of illiterate Spanish immigrants, so there's not much that's elegant about me. I don't have it in the genes, at least not from my father's side."

Yet to judge by his mannerisms, speech, and a face that

preserves many of the features that his son had in his youth, there's a lot of Roberto in León and vice versa.

For example, Roberto's adventurous soul is inherited from his father, who left home when he was nineteen to live in Valparaíso. Roberto's grandfather had died when León was sixteen—from a "massive heart attack," of course.

León spent two years in the Chilean Navy until, sick of following orders, he sent them, he says, "all to hell." After that he went to Santiago, where he met the primary school teacher Victoria Ávalos. He married her and they had Roberto in 1953, followed by a daughter, María Salomé, in 1954. "He was my favorite, more than the daughter I had with the same mother," the father admits.[1]

Many years later, after Roberto and León had both died, María Salomé, in an interview, would twist her face into an expression of bitterness and frank hostility when the conversation turned to her father. It was a complicated family.

When the family lived in Valparaíso, a city of hills, León worked as a truck driver for the INSA tire factory. Their home was in Los Placeres, at Calle Mercedes 24. "Roberto used to say: 'I'm from number 24 Metal Street,' when he was little," León remembers.

The old man grows emotional and his eyes well up when he remembers what he felt when he read the story "Last Evenings on Earth" for the first time. The story is about a trip he took with his son to Acapulco in the 1980s. "That's how it was, exactly how he tells it in the book," León says.[2]

Much has been said about the estrangement between father and son that led to a silence between them lasting almost two decades. However, there is evidence to show that the bond between Roberto and León was much closer than the hasty obituaries written in the heat—or cold—of the death of the writer tended to allow.

León Bolaño was, after all, a standoffish but good man. This is affirmed by Jaime Quezada, the Chilean poet who spent a year with the family in Mexico City. "It's not easy to tell from his facial expression or smile whether he's in a good or bad mood. In any case, a very intimate goodness or tenderness seems to make him recoil from the world, giving outsiders the impression of distance or aloofness."[3]

"We had a very good relationship. He loved me a lot and I loved him," León says, referring to his son.

It was his mother, Victoria, who left Roberto in Mexico when she decided to separate from her husband and leave for Spain, taking María Salomé with her. The dysfunctional relationship in the Bolaño-Ávalos marriage, between two contrasting spirits and strong, independent characters, came to an end thanks to what León Bolaño describes as a "misunderstanding."

LEÓN BOLAÑO: It was dinnertime and there was a Colombian girl, a friend of my wife's, there. When I called them to come to the table, the girl, who was quite angry, said that she wasn't going to eat and was leaving. Then she asked Roberto for a book she had given him when she arrived. I had seen her give it to him. "You want me to give back the book you gave me?" Roberto asked. Annoyed, I got involved and told him to give it back, saying that I'd get him another. The problem was that we kept on arguing and I ended up throwing the young woman out. My wife came and said: "If she leaves, I'm going too." And that was why we separated, because I was defending Roberto.

The union seems only to have left deep bitterness, at least on León's side. He refers to Victoria Ávalos often as simply "that woman," criticizing her for "spending a lot and ruining me," among other complaints.

When Roberto's mother and sister left for Spain, father and son stayed in the house in Guadalupe Tepeyac, living there alone. By that time, León was working at the Pascual food company, which in the 1980s became a cooperative after a long labor conflict that Roberto's father didn't want any part of. This was where he started out on the path to becoming an independent salesman, first selling cigarettes to stores he knew and then opening his own shop.

When I met him, the old man spoke from a sofa in his living room. His house was in Cadereyta de Montes, a Mexican town in Querétaro with its share of wood and marble workers, where most of the population works in trade or agriculture.

On one of the streets, a sign hangs over a modest corner store: "EL CHILENO" (The Chilean), the fruit of the efforts of León Bolaño and his second wife, Irene, the parents of three siblings Roberto never met in person, although in his final years he spoke to them over the telephone quite regularly.

They started out selling soaps, salami, eggs, and cold cuts until they forced their way into the middle class thanks to the construction of the hydroelectric power station at Infiernillo Canyon, near the store.

"The construction of the dam was an opportunity … It was really very good for us," says León.

In 1977, Roberto left Mexico for Spain, never to return. He toured France and North Africa and found work in Spain as a dishwasher, doing maintenance work at a campground, and garbage collector, before settling in the coastal city of Blanes in 1981. After he left, father and son were in and out of touch, but León recalls: "We spoke about all kinds of things. He often remembered his horse in Chile. He remembered how he and María Salomé once fell off a horse and she screamed much louder than he did."

He doesn't much like to remember his professional boxing

career (his nickname was "Golden Fists"). "I retired because I said to myself: 'I have to educate my children or I'll go crazy.' At the end of a boxing career, you end up stupid and start to talk nonsense," he says. He had learned the secrets of pugilism in the navy and fought in a few professional fights in Los Ángeles, all of which he won by a knockout in the first round.

León Bolaño, who was a well-built middleweight, ate like an athlete and was sometimes covered in the local sports press. He says that Roberto inherited his confrontational attitude and bravery from him. To prove it, he has in his possession a log book from his time in the navy in Chile. It is full of censures, he says, for showing a lack of respect to an officer, for "hitting an officer" and "for things like that."

"Roberto had a lot of balls. He never gave up. He was incredible," León says. "Have you read his interviews on the Internet? He gave the journalists a kick up the ass. He practically called them *huevones* [idiots], as they say in Chile. He had a strong character and saw things very clearly."

León Bolaño's portrayal of a brave, irrepressible man is unwittingly backed up by his ex-wife, Victoria Ávalos. In 2006, she told the Chilean journalist Patricio Jara, "Roberto was very brave and didn't bow down to anyone."

When in his last interview Bolaño was asked to describe what Latin American scenes came to mind, one of his answers was: "My father's truck broken down on a desert road."

The father remembers this too: "When we lived in Valparaíso, I had a big thirty-ton truck, and on the journey, before we got to La Serena, an injection pump blew out."

LEÓN BOLAÑO: Fucking hell, what a problem. I was alone in my truck with my kid. Roberto would have been about four years old. We were alone in the middle of the desert. Fortunately a friend passed by and I asked him to get a mechanic. He was an Italian who always fixed my truck when I was on the road. I only had a little water. Roberto would say he was thirsty and I'd give him some water. Then he'd ask, "Aren't you going to drink?" I wasn't, I was worried it would run out. Suddenly I saw smoke off in the distance. It was a house, a very humble one. I gave the lady there a forty-kilo bag of flour and she made some bread. We ate that for three days until the mechanic arrived. Then we started out on our journey again. My son was asleep in the cabin when suddenly something flew very fast right over the truck. It was an army mail plane that landed on the sand. They used the truck as a marker to land. I was terrified and Roberto cried a lot. Imagine: a plane flying that close to you!

A lover of tango, León Bolaño was a great dancer. He liked Hugo del Carril and loved Carlos Gardel. He said that he owed nothing to life and had never had a bad time in his long existence.

"My son was a good son," he says. "He greeted everyone very politely. Guadalupe Tepeyac was full of hippies who got him into marijuana and that kind of thing. I said to him: 'Roberto, don't get involved with those people.' And he answered: 'Don't worry, Papa, there won't be any trouble.' Roberto was never a drug addict! He just met with his friends to drink coffee, write, and exchange ideas."

•   •   •

Alcira, the woman León Bolaño blamed for the breakup of his marriage, was a great friend of Roberto's mother. She would come to the house at Guadalupe Tepeyac and stay there for a few days before disappearing for months at a time.

Her full name was Alcira Soust Scaffo. She was a Uruguayan teacher (not Colombian, as León Bolaño thought) who went to Mexico and met Bolaño in 1970. She inspired *Amulet*, the story of Auxilio Lacouture, a woman who locks herself in the Humanities Building during an army raid on UNAM. The character first appeared in *The Savage Detectives*.

The young Uruguayan literary critic Ignacio Bajter wrote a long article in the cultural journal *Brecha* in which he reports that Soust Scaffo went to Mexico in 1952 when she was twenty-nine and lived there for thirty-six years.

BAJTER: Bolaño didn't see Alcira [Soust Scaffo] again after 1976. His sister Salomé might have talked to him about her. In Catalonia, he wrote *The Savage Detectives*, which was published in 1998. But the voice of the character Auxilio Lacouture stayed with him and obliged the writer to lengthen the short monologue from the book into the manuscript for *Amulet*: a musical novel for just one instrument that was to be the first installment of an unfinished trilogy, which Bolaño continued with *By Night in Chile*. They are theatrical pieces with a single, unstable, flighty voice trapped in a dialogue with their fate. The fate chosen for the protagonist of *Amulet* was that of someone who has given up everything to lose themselves in the poetry and the horror. People say that Alcira used to complain: "That damn Bolaño! Why won't he leave me out of his books?" This supposed reluctance to be portrayed by Bolaño is just an orthodox fantasy of post-infrarradicalism: Alcira disappeared the moment her image was reflected in the mirror of fiction.

"She was around forty and always wore the same clothes," remembers the Chilean Victoria Soto, another friend of the Bolaño family. "She dressed like a hippie. She was very intelligent, worked at the university, and translated lots of French writers. That's how I met her. She was just like the protagonist of *Amulet*, which was so, so true to real life. He wrote her in the first person and that's how Alcira was, fantastic."

Roberto's mother's friends, Alcira and Victoria, were for the adolescent in Guadalupe Tepeyac strong female characters with whom he enjoyed spending time, as he didn't seem to have much fun with people his age.

It seems Bolaño built paternal relationships with his elders, employing the sense of humor for which he would later become so celebrated.

"Once I was going out with a divorced guy, I was walking and turned to speak to some friends. I stepped to one side and a bullet shot past me and broke a window. If I hadn't moved, it would have killed me," remembers Victoria Soto. "Roberto said to me: 'You know what? It's obvious that the ex-wife has taken a hit out on you.' He wasn't at all alarmed. He had an incredible sense of humor. He always had an anecdote to tell and always saw good things in people."

Victoria Soto, like Alcira, was friends with Victoria first and then Roberto, who was several years younger than her. In an interview, she describes meeting Victoria by chance in Mexico City:

> SOTO: I went to Mexico as part of an exchange between Latin American universities. I came to give a month's seminar, but a month is a very short period of time to get to know this marvelous country, so I decided to stay. When my money ran out, after I stopped being a tourist, I had to look for work. I stopped a guy in the street to ask the way somewhere and he asked if I was Chilean and said that there were a few Chileans where he

worked: "The manager is Chilean, there are some Chilean secre-
taries ..." I went the next day, and the day after that started work.
Victoria Ávalos was there ... We made friends immediately. At
first we were poor, we drank a Coca-Cola between the two of
us at lunchtime and bought some bread to go with it. That was
all we could afford, but we were happy. I remember those times
very well.[4]

In her free time, she goes on to say, she typed up Roberto's hand-
written manuscripts. He had terrible handwriting and used to
give her unfinished stories that, as was to be expected, made him
unbearably anxious.

"He was about sixteen and wrote little novels, there was always something interesting in them, strange characters and such,"
she says. "I loved to read them. His father used to say that Roberto needed to find work. I'd reply that writing was his work.
His father didn't understand that that was work too, even if it
wasn't paid. Victoria used to argue with her husband over things
like that."

Soto says that Roberto was a nice teenager, pleasant to talk
to, and treated adults as though he were actually older than them.
He also had an excellent relationship at the time with his sister,
María Salomé. "When I went to their house for the first time, he
was with María Salomé," she recalls. "I went in to drop off my bag
and he opened the door for me. Brother and sister were both right
there. I flew in in a terrible hurry, and he looked at me smiling,
that was how Roberto was, always looking crafty. I asked if they
were Victoria's children. This was the first time I met them. His
mother said that Roberto was a very intelligent boy and that he
knew how to read and write when he was three, something she
couldn't explain."

She also reports that the adolescent Roberto loved to walk

the streets in the center of Mexico City and took photos of himself with the street vendors. He was egocentric, wore glasses that he barely needed, and always adopted an intellectual pose.

"I didn't pry into his private life. It seems that he didn't want anything, he didn't want to talk about or explain anything, like all depressed people," she says. "He suffered terrible fits of depression. Sometimes it made me sad to see him. I came to see him and he didn't look at me, didn't greet me, or anything like that. Then he'd say: 'Let's go out for a walk.' He wanted to introduce me to a writer friend of his, but nothing happened. Then an engineer came by and he said: 'That one's for you, every time I see him I say to myself that he's just right for Vicky,' but I stayed single."

·   ·   ·

As for Roberto's romantic life in Mexico City, Victoria Soto says: "He was so in love with Lisa, he told me that he had met a girl who was so pretty, so lovely, that he was already in love. Lisa moved in with him at home. She was sixteen or seventeen." She remembers: "His mother rearranged the room so that they could be together. Victoria had a very open mind and supported her son in almost everything."[5] Soto also remembers his close friendship with the Mexican poet Mario Santiago Papasquiaro: "Santiago was like his brother, they communicated very well, did the same things, and spoke the same language." And she has this to say about Roberto's mother: "Victoria was a very intellectual woman, very political, with a lot of interests. She was a wonderful woman, generous, pretty, and hardworking. Strangely, my friendship with Victoria actually led to me growing closer to Roberto."

Soto and Bolaño drifted apart in later years, but she regrets that the relationship didn't last longer.

SOTO: I saw him again when he was in his twenties ... I was very happy to see him, I had my baby with me and asked him who he looked like, and he said that at that age babies don't look like anyone.

He went to bed very late and always said to me that before writing, before he was even thinking, he was already writing, that something very strange happened to him. The pen moved before he could come up with the phrases, it was very odd. María Salomé told me that their mother believed all that, though she didn't and I shouldn't listen to him.

I knew Bolaño for a short but intense time at the beginning of the 1970s ... Bolaño was quiet, alert with a harsh black humor, and I liked him immediately. He was seven years younger than me. I saw him as a youngster, but even now I think that twenty years is nothing and my best friends are younger than forty. We used to go to La Habana Café, to another café that's not there anymore, and to the cantinas for long nights of beer and tequila. When we talked about poetry, Bolaño was the best person to talk to. We had Whitman behind us and Vallejo in front, with the extraordinary range of contemporary Peruvian poetry as our companions. I told him about the poets from Hora Zero who had been my friends in Lima, I talked passionately about Negro Verástegui and loaned him books by Pimentel. Bolañito was timid but profound. I lost track of him in '72 and never saw him again. I think that he quietly went back to Chile while I went to the United States. I missed the Infrarealist performances that caused so much fuss years later. It was a shame, he would have been a dear friend. I now know that he still remembered our meetings years later, after the year 2000, just as I remember them. In spite of all the good and bad that the industry does to us, we're both still just adolescents dreaming of riding black motorcycles down a highway, dreaming of ephemeral but eternal love, with our broken dream of a world capable of passing from darkness into the light. That's what his writing has, both his poetry and prose: it doesn't bore you, perhaps because he wrote it with body and mind. He wrote uncompromisingly, facing up to an industry that tried to swallow him whole, like the poet that he was and is. Simple and honest, faithful to his beliefs; that's how I see Bolañito ... I liked Bolaño's pregnant silence, I liked his sense of humor and his savage detective's air of concentration, I liked his observations and his occasionally brusque presence ... I'd have liked to have seen him and given him a big hug after we had finally grown up.

4

The First Publisher

A painful death—225 books, 225 Cards—A book by Borges—A book by Ezra Pound

"Juan Pascoe has created a monumental body of work. He has re-imagined the life and work of some of the first Mexican printers; his hope-filled homage to the book in times of violence and cholera, demonstrating his instinct for uncovering new poets, his acceptance of the new opportunities presented by the computer and the Internet, and his love for centuries-old arts nonetheless looks toward the future," wrote Carmen Boullosa in her column in the *El Universal* newspaper.

She is describing a "gringo" who has become fully integrated into Mexican culture, perhaps one of the most beloved figures in the diffuse universe of underground poets and Bohemians: Juan Pascoe, a major publisher of poetry.

It is a matter of historical record that Pascoe was Roberto Bolaño's first publisher. Bolaño met Pascoe through Pascoe's brother Ricardo and his sister-in-law, the artist Carla Rippey. He remembers Bolaño as a very dear friend, perhaps because "the friendships we make in our youth are usually the strongest." Although he last saw him in 1976, he continued to exchange letters with the writer and still felt very close to him.

Bolaño's unexpected death in 2003 hit him "very hard." When he heard the news, his first impulse was to print something. To Juan, printing is an act that follows and completes writing. He called Carla Rippey, who remembered a poem by Bolaño that Mario Santiago had left her. Santiago used to visit his friends' houses with letters and books that he left for them, and took away with him—perhaps never to return—other letters and books. Pascoe made 225 cards with a fragment of that poem by Bolaño, which was the same figure as the number of copies he printed of *Reinventar el amor* (Reinventing Love), Bolaño's first book, a collection of poetry, in 1976—a book that was published when he was just twenty-three.

Most of these cards went to Bolaño's wife. Juan gave another pile of cards to Carmen Boullosa to disperse in New York, and he kept some to give to people who came to his enormous house in Michoacán, where he has lived in complete harmony with the land in a village called Tacámbaro since 1981, surrounded by the printing machines that belonged to his now-legendary Martín Pescador press. The poem that Pascoe printed is called "Lanzallamas" (Flamethrower).

PASCOE: When, thirty years ago now, we published the collection *Reinventar el amor*, Roberto said to me: "One day you'll be very proud to have brought out this book." And I am, although any poet might have said the same thing at the time. I barely sold a copy of this book, his friends were poor and stole books rather than buying them. He came to my house and asked me to give him a few copies, and I gave them to him. Two weeks later, he came back for more, and so on.

Roberto would come and go from the press, which at the time was in the Mixcoac neighborhood. He worked on a drinks delivery truck that made its way through the villages of Morelos. The roads weren't asphalted, they were dusty paths, and Roberto, who was very young, would travel on top of the truck.

The other day I went to Oaxaca to see Jan Hendrix, a Dutch artist living there, and the conversation turned to Roberto. Jan said to me: "Roberto was a little irritable and aggressive, wasn't he?" I said that was true. I never experienced that aggressiveness, however, mainly because I was a relative of Carla and Ricardo, whom he loved. Also, I had a press, so I was his perfect companion. I became less perfect when I started publishing some books by "Pazist" poets he didn't like.

It was Roberto who more or less chose the name of the press from a list another poet had brought me. It was Roberto who introduced me to Efraín Huerta, and I left his house with a poetry collection under my arm for publication. We weren't great buddies, Bolaño's only buddies were Bruno Montané and Mario Santiago, but we had a significant literary connection. When he didn't write to me, he sent me messages through Carla. He wanted to know if I was in love, if the press was going well, that kind of thing.

In July 1977, Bolaño wrote to Pascoe to talk of the poetry he was writing in Spain. It was an era, Bolaño wrote, in which the remains of Infrarealism had moved to the diaspora, but he wanted Pascoe to know he was still writing, still thinking about writing. That Bolaño would write to Pascoe about the status of the Infrarealism movement isn't suprising—Pascoe had witnessed its origin.

PASCOE: I remember the night that Infrarealism was founded at the Montanés' apartment. It was full of people. Roberto was the leader, he was sitting at a table very formally. The speeches started and I didn't understand a thing, so I distracted myself with shapes the smoke from Roberto's cigarette was making in the air. I'd gone with my brother Ricardo and Carla. We took the trolley to the city center where the Montanés lived. Everyone said, "The Infrarealist movement has begun"—I can't remember if we signed a piece of paper or not—and then we left.

No one asked me if I wanted to be an Infrarealist. I was the friend of the boss, so they took it for granted. Although I really wasn't much competition for the poets. I was of dubious nationality, I liked the Mexican folk music that Roberto deplored, and was fascinated by typography. I was a strange guy. As Francisco Segovia says: "Everyone knows about Juan Pascoe's quirks."

He didn't just steal books from bookshops. When he came to my house he scanned the shelves. I remember once having found a very valuable edition of *Orlando* by Virginia Woolf, a first edition from 1937 translated by Jorge Luis Borges. I showed it to Roberto very enthusiastically and he said to me: "Well, good, I'll take it with me. I know someone who should read this book." He didn't say who. And he took it. Of course, he never gave it back. I should say, to be fair to him, that he gave me a copy of *The Pisan Cantos* by Ezra Pound, José Vázquez Amaral's translation, and I felt well compensated.

• • •

In Paolo Sorrentino's 2008 film *Il Divo,* Giulio Andreotti, masterfully portrayed by Toni Servillo, complains to a colleague when, during his fall from grace amid a series of lawsuits linking him to the Cosa Nostra, the man who was elected prime minister of his country seven times finds himself being stripped of past honors:

Do you know what really upsets me? They've removed me from the presidency of the Musical Circle. Next they'll throw me out of the Institute of Ciceronian Studies, they might even take away my Honoris Causa degrees. It isn't vanity. I come from the countryside, I was poor. To me, cultural legitimacy has always been more important than politics. I've always preferred it when people describe me as a cultured man rather than a great statesman.

The short or long life of Bolaño, depending on how you look at it, and his drive to transcend his social class, which he regarded with a certain indifference, would seem to agree with these sentiments perfectly. Bolaño didn't have noble titles, money, or cars (he couldn't even drive), and seemed determined to complete his education with a voracious discipline and insatiable desire for literary knowledge that, like many other writers, couldn't be satisfied by obeying familial strictures at home, and certainly not at school.

The arrogance that could be confused with conceitedness was, in truth, a pride in what he had achieved on his own. "Not in my worst fits of drunkenness did my lucidity dip below a certain level, a sense of prosody and rhythm, a certain horror of plagiarism, mediocrity, and silence," said Bolaño, referring to certain authors he believed to be inferior such as Ángeles Mastretta and especially his compatriots Isabel Allende and Marcela Serrano.

As a man who didn't have much and wasn't interested in material goods, Bolaño seemed to have been born to fulfill a mission of self-enlightenment from an early age.

"In Chile, when he was little, he was already starting to write. Working hard to prepare himself, he read a lot, a lot. The school often got in contact with us because he would talk back to the teacher. He'd often tell them that they were wrong. Then the teacher would say to me that my son was right, but 'tell your son not to say so in front of the others because it makes the teacher look ridiculous,'" remembers León Bolaño, discussing his son's behavior at school in Los Ángeles.

When the family went to Mexico, Roberto went to a religious school at Ferrocarril Hidalgo, but wasn't there for long. According to his father, the priests threw him out because of the same know-it-all attitude that had caused so much trouble in the school in Chile. After 1968, he would never again set foot in a classroom—his education in literature and politics was al-most entirely self-taught.

"He was a very studious boy. On Sundays we went to the Gigante [now called Soriana] on the road to Guadalupe. Roberto would say to me: 'Look, Papa, go and buy whatever you're going to buy and I'll stay here to read books.' When I came back from shopping he'd read about four books," León said, exaggerating as a proud father does.

Roberto's father described him as a very unusual boy who liked to take walks and had no interest in money at all: "He wrote short stories for the *Excélsior* and *El Mercurio* and gave me their checks to deal with. Sometimes I gave him five pesos and he said to me: 'No, that's too much, give me two.' At that time, the bus cost thirty cents. Of course, sometimes I had to pay the bill at the taco stand. There'd be nothing to eat at home because I left very early and didn't come back all day. So Roberto would go to the taco stall on the road to Guadalupe and eat beans and tacos."

5

The Origins of the Infrarealists

What we did was annoy everyone—Send Bolaño back to Santiago; Santiago too—A punch-up, of course—We went to the same parties but sat at different tables—A kind of revelation—The Infras weren't writers—You're a member of the Infrarealists—Cadaver eaters—A dogfight—The poet "Ladín" Cerda has sold out—He was holding court—If you're not with me, you're against me—Like Bukowski—It's envy

The notorious Infrarealist literary movement, with which Bolaño would be deeply identified thoughout his life, was founded at the start of 1976 in the home of a Chilean poet and close friend of Bolaño's, Bruno Montané. He appears in *The Savage Detectives* as the character Felipe Müller. Born in Santiago de Chile in 1957, Bruno is the brother of the painter Álvaro Montané.

Bruno left Chile in 1974, at seventeen, after the military coup had put his father, an archaeologist, out of work. Montané's parents still live in Sonora, a city in the north of Mexico where the third part of *The Savage Detectives* is set, where they moved after living for a period in Mexico City.

Bruno met Bolaño, who had by then been living in Mexico for six years, through Jaime Quezada, who gave him the Montané brothers' address in Mexico City. They immediately hit it off and started to publish things together. First came an anthology of young Chilean poets with the help of a former Spanish Republican exiled in Mexico, Juan Rejano, who also appears briefly in the *The Savage Detectives*. Then they published their first poems in *El Nacional*, whose cultural supplement was run by Rejano.

Thinking back, Bruno especially remembers the close friendship between Bolaño and Mario Santiago, whom Bolaño called "the best poet I ever met ... an amazing talent."[1] Santiago and Bolaño met at La Habana Café in 1975: "We were all very innocent, adolescents who knew something about a few things and nothing about a lot more."[2]

Montané also remembers what the poet Nicanor Parra meant to Roberto in these days: "*Obra gruesa* [Heavy Work] was his touchstone."[3] He also remembers that Roberto read a lot of science fiction and noir and that they burned Bolaño's convoluted theatrical works together, at Bolaño's own urging, "because he said that they were awful."[4]

In an interview on the Chilean television program *Off the Record*, Bolaño remembered the origins of the Infrarealist movement this way:

BOLAÑO: Mario Santiago and I founded Infrarealism. At the time we were pretty irresponsible and our theoretical arguments were fairly incoherent. Essentially, what annoyed many people in the Mexican literary establishment was that we weren't aligned with any of the cliques, or powerful groups. In Mexican literature there had always been groups of warriors and their samurai. We weren't with any of them. We weren't with the left; it was a Stalinist, dogmatic, authoritarian left. A horrible left. Neither were we with the elegant right, which wasn't elegant at all. Theirs was a moth-eaten elegance. We weren't with the avant-garde who were only interested in earning money and whose idea of the avant-garde was stuck far in the past. What we did was annoy everyone. I remember that someone, in a moment of great inspiration, their only moment of great inspiration, published a text that said: "SEND BOLAÑO BACK TO SANTIAGO; SANTIAGO TOO."[5] They couldn't stand us in Mexico, it was complete and utter hatred, they didn't like us at all. That was who the Infrarealists were. Then I left for Spain and never went back to Mexico. In contrast, Mario, who spent some time living in Europe and the Middle East, went back. They made him pay dearly for it. Now that he's dead, lots of people are coming out of the woodwork to say that he was a great poet, but they waited until he was dead to say so. I feel embarrassed about my work from that time, almost as though it were written by another writer, because I've changed as a poet and a writer. There was one great poet in that group, Mario Santiago, while I was the agitator. Of course, Mario Santiago was much more of an agitator than I was, but I wasn't even close to him as poet. My move to Europe changed my perspective on my poetry.[6]

In actuality, Bolaño rarely spoke about his Infrarealist period, although he used it at length—and presented it to the world—in *The Savage Detectives*, in which his former comrades in arms were called "realvisceralistas."

Apart from Santiago and Montané, the group also included Rubén Medina ("Rafael Barrios" in the novel), a Mexican poet and professor who now lives in the United States.

"Infrarealism posed a very important ethical challenge," says Medina. "Aesthetics became secondary, the most important issues were ethical. These ethics were expressed by taking a strategic, critical poetic position on the margins." He believes that the Infrarealist position was something that Bolaño maintained throughout his life. This affirmation contradicts other scholars of Latin American literature such as Jorge Volpi, who doesn't see Infrarealism as an important factor in Bolaño's work.

What Medina is saying is that the Infrarealist influence on Bolaño can be seen in his attitude to life and his writing career, not his literary aesthetic. This is also the position of the critic Ignacio Echevarría, who coordinated an event paying homage to Bolaño in Madrid and invited Medina to speak.

ECHEVARRÍA: Bolaño was a little-known writer until the start of the nineties. It was only after '96 that he started to get a foothold in the publishing market. In the eighties and the early nineties he basically led the same life that he had had in Mexico. He had minor jobs to keep himself afloat, had enough to eat, a place to sleep, could go to the cinema, drink a beer and write, write, and write.

Infrarealism was founded during a series of meetings between several young, very, very young poets brought together by certain principles, a common interest and acceptance of other poetics. Infrarealism is a form of approaching the abyss in a way that writers don't tend to, it is a way of exploring, of writing poetry, a way to screw with your fellow man.

MEDINA: We disrupted recitals, we didn't want civilized confrontations in which our poetry competed, where one person would read, and then the other would read their stuff and the audience or critics would adjudicate. We thought that that was just recirculating power. We used guerrilla tactics: we'd arrive, act, and then hide. When Bolaño started to gain some recognition, suddenly people who had bad-mouthed Infrarealism started to be more careful about what they said: one of its members had, almost inexplicably, managed to produce an incredible body of work. Let's say that for me Infrarealism was an adventure, an ethical position that set us apart, even though we weren't a tight-knit group.

Bolaño was less effusive about his youthful activities, downplaying the movement by narrowing its years of activity.

BOLAÑO: Infrarealism was a movement that Roberto Matta created when Breton threw him out of the Surrealists. It lasted three years. There was just one person, Matta, in the group. Years later, Infrarealism would rise again in Mexico with a group of Mexican poets plus two Chilean ones. It was a kind of group Dadaism that organized fairly rambunctious events. At one point there were a lot of members, about fifty people, of whom in truth only two or three were really worth anything as poets. When Mario Santiago and I went off to Europe, the movement ended. Those who stayed in Mexico couldn't keep it going. That was because, really, Infrarealism was a madness that Mario and I shared. It lasted between '75 and '77.[7]

Medina, however, says, "Bolaño never discarded the ethics of Infrarealism. He might say: 'Infrarealism is over, Infrarealism is Mario Santiago and I,' but all his literature is related to marginalization, the figure of the writer, with black holes. What is *2666* if not a big black hole of humanity, crime and horror? How can this evil be understood? Roberto brings readers closer to the black holes, which are an Infrarealist concept. It's in Roberto Bolaño's manifesto."[8]

But what was Infrarealism exactly? In Bolaño's "Infrarealist Manifesto," he evokes the clichéd perception of the literary universe as an immense "ocean of nothingness." But what if, the manifesto asks, on the "celestial maps, like the maps of earth, only the star-cities are shown while the star-villages are omitted?" What if there is much more than meets the eye? What if we have to fight for new perspectives and visions—especially in the literary world? In the unorthodox, stream-of-conscious manifesto, Bolaño goes on to compare his new group to snipers and boys who smash up cafés and freak out at the supermarket, and he outlines an active position for poets: they should be heroes, and they should help reveal other heroes." He writes: "Our ethic is the Revolution, our aesthetic is Life: one-and-the-same."

Medina says that Bolaño never "discarded that ethical position, none of us did. He was a poet with a great metaphorical drive. Over the years he discarded the metaphors and the poems became more direct, less metaphorical, and had more narrative.

In fact, his poems started to become almost a less fictional kind of narrative prose."

"In his fiction, he creates, he plays, playing a lot of tricks on the reader, giving them a lot of clues and using a lot of misdirection," he says. "If the reader wants to build up an image of Roberto through certain autobiographical elements in his fiction, it becomes a never-ending game involving lots of different characteristics and Bolaños. If you look at the poetry there's this guy who works as a campsite manager and goes to Barcelona one night, goes into a bar alone and thinks about Mexico: that's Bolaño, just as he is," says Medina. It is this image, he reflects, that Bolaño created of himself during the period in Mexico.

MEDINA: You could go to La Habana Café and tell him something, and then another five people would come in and there'd be six or seven of us, and Roberto would tell them what you just told them but in a fictionalized way. He had a great knack for telling stories. My first sight of Roberto was at La Casa del Lago at a gig. There was a guy standing at the back, dressed in black with long hair, smoking as though he'd been condemned to life in prison. When I saw him I thought that he looked ten years older than me. Later I found out that it was just two or three. When I met him, I found that he had a great intellectual maturity and a great capacity for reading, he read everything. He wrote down everything he wanted to do clearly in an agenda. He was playful, good company.

I very much enjoy reading Roberto, I like him as a poet, I like him as a narrator. He left a great burden on the Infrarealists because he built the Infrarealists as a literary construct and we have to do something about it because in a way it's his joke, as though he's saying, "Come on, you bastards," declaring a sort of marginalization.

The utopian failure we dreamed of with Infrarealism can be found in Bolaño's literature.

Though the giants of the Infrarealist movement are dead, "the Infrarealist movement in the twenty-first century still has the rebellious energy that gave rise to it, publications on two continents, enough unpublished work for dozens of volumes, fame in five or more foreign countries, and, of course, the aura of silence and denial that official culture in Mexico has imposed because of the legend of black suns that surrounds these insurrectionist poets," writes José Ramón Méndez Estrada, the brother of the deceased poet Cuauhtémoc Méndez, another poet involved with the founding of the Infrarealist movement.[9]

Méndez believes it was Infrarealism that inspired Bolaño and not the other way around. In his view, Bolaño had spent his time in Mexico getting to know the stories of the poets, putting them in a novel and then becoming rich and famous with his work.

Méndez met Bolaño one drunken night when the tequila had run out and Mario Santiago invited him to come to a friend's house. They got to the apartment in the city center, close to the Reloj Chino and the Monument to the Revolution, where Roberto lived briefly before leaving for Spain. It was about four in the morning.

MÉNDEZ: Mario took me to Roberto's apartment because he would supposedly have something to drink. When we rang the bell, Roberto answered, I didn't know him. He was angry because we'd interrupted his early morning writing. He didn't give us a warm welcome but he let us in. Once inside, having heard about our predicament, he took out a bottle of sweet wine, or vermouth, I don't know what it was. He had a glass with us almost out of politeness and then made himself some coffee.[10]

We started to talk about lots of things, poetry at the time, the poetry by the kids in Peru, the Beatniks and what we were doing in what was left of the workshop run by Juan Bañuelos.[11] Roberto got excited during the conversation and eventually was very happy that we had spoken. We left the house at dawn and as we said farewell he said to us: "You're the Beatniks. You're [Mario Santiago] Allen Ginsberg and he's [Méndez] Gregory Corso."[12]

A few months later, Mario broke the news that we were going to start the Infrarealist movement. It was Roberto's suggestion. He had found the path to fame and the bards to inspire him. At the end of the day he liked to write novels about poets, didn't he? That's why he came to us, looking for interesting subjects.

To do that he got up early, at about four in the morning, to write four or five verses until eight. Verses that were to make him famous, something that he eventually achieved. I suppose that later on he wrote more than five verses a day. We were friends for a while, until he got angry because I called him a bureaucrat rather than an artist. We never spoke again.

He liked my poems. I once confessed to him that the inspiration for one of my verses came from a phrase that Roberto had said: "Children are born to be happy." And I put it in a poem. "Ah, did I really say that," he replied. That showed me that he didn't pay attention to what he was saying.

Before Roberto went to Spain, he brought out the book *Muchachos desnudos bajo el arcoíris de fuego* [Naked Boys Under the Rainbow of Fire] and the magazine *Correspondencia infra* [Infra Correspondence]. I don't know who chose the texts for it, but I was excluded. When he had a page in the cultural supplement of *El Día*, "El gallo ilustrado," he printed something of mine.[13] I still thought of myself as part of the movement he invented and which he later renounced.

The Savage Detectives is good, it's entertaining in spite of its structural and technical flaws. It's a good read. It's nonetheless a complete exaggeration to compare Roberto to Lezama Lima or Cortázar, or even Cervantes. He's a good writer of fiction, without a doubt, but is perhaps overrated. The novel's link to real events meant that it got more attention, but that was his strategy to become famous. Now he's where he wanted to be, his work will be discussed for a long time. Bolaño strategically plots his fame outside of official culture. I haven't read *2666*, I haven't been able to afford such an expensive book or found anyone to lend it to me, but a friend of mine says that it is very critical of academia. I don't know what Bolaño's education was, because he always boasted about being self-taught. He certainly knew how to read.

Méndez insists on describing Infrarealism as an attitude rather than a determined position on certain subjects, given that all the members were different from one another: "We didn't think the same way about anything, not women or politics, for example. What brought us together was the desire to blow out the brains of the official culture that was and still is doing us so much damage, those literati, men of letters, who don't work or study. All they do is harm the language."

• • •

"My relationship with Bolaño goes back to our adolescence, the first years of youth when I was still in school and had stopped wanting to be a fireman and astronaut and started to want to be a painter, poet, or filmmaker," says the poet and writer José María Espinasa. "In 1976, Mexico City had fifteen million inhabitants, but we apprentice poets all knew each other. We went to the same launches, the same parties, and it was inevitable that we'd start to interact. I think that I must have seen Roberto seven or eight times, and we always ended up arguing, which was a constant occurrence at the time, and the arguments I refer to involved punch-ups, of course."[14]

Espinasa's description of his fights with Bolaño sounds like a scene from Monty Python. On one side was "Roberto behind the poets who supported him, and the other me, behind the poets who supported me. Courage wasn't one of the Infrarealists' virtues," he says.[15]

> ESPINASA: I saw him especially at La Habana Café, we sat at different tables. I knew some of the members of the Casa del Lago who went on to become part of the Infrarealist movement. We had ongoing arguments. The group I belonged to was in almost mystical awe of Octavio Paz. The Infrarealists, in contrast, objected to him with an iconoclastic belligerence that was also somewhat mystical and also the result of enormous admiration. The authors we liked from outside Mexico were pretty much the same, we could recite Ungaretti or Jaime Gil de Biedma almost from memory, and that allowed us to establish a complicity that was almost beyond the rivalries. There were also the traditional struggles for the favors of the girls of the time, the friends who came with us to those parties, who accompanied us on that adventure.

José María Espinasa lost track of Roberto and Bruno Montané when they left Mexico City, but he continued to see Mario Santiago.

> ESPINASA: I think that when Roberto left, the group broke up. Its aura remained but it slowly faded until the appearance of

The Savage Detectives, which gave rise to, how shall I say it, something that was more mythical than real.

To me, the real Roberto is the one from the stories. The big-river novels he published are full of perfect stories, but as novels they don't achieve what they set out to do. Of course, it's very difficult to debate these things when dealing with an author with whom it is difficult to separate the textual value from its context, the sentimental value from its myth. What is unusual is that the seductive quality he had at twenty remained throughout his life and now even after his death.

The Roberto I knew was a young man with long hair and a smile that went from ear to ear. The one I see in the photos that circulated after his death was a far more melancholic Roberto, and I think that in general the friends he had here became more melancholy. Carla Rippey's artwork, the editorial approach of Juan Pascoe, who was his first editor and publisher, continued with the urban underclass of Infrarealist poets. The writer who became a superstar of Latin American literature and the friend from our youth and adolescence don't seem to fit together for me. Maybe I've unconsciously tried to keep them separate, unmixed, and thus preserve a lasting affection for them both.

In the group of writers that formed first *Cuadernos de Literatura* [Literary Notes] and then the magazine *Anábasis*, there was undoubtedly an admiration for Paz but there was also quite a strong critical tone. There were other groups, like the one that produced the magazine *El Zaguán*,[16] who were much more admiring. Among them all, the admiration for Efraín Huerta arose from the conviction that poetry had to be more immediate, more critical of the present time, more direct, less intellectually convoluted, but looking back thirty years later, all that seems very problematic.

How could you call a poet like Mario Santiago an anti-intellectual when he wrote a poem called "From a Student of Heidegger to a Follower of Karl Marx," or something like that? Listen, reading Heidegger doesn't exactly translate to an immediate, savage poetry.

The people who were part of *Cuadernos de Literatura* or the Martín Pescador workshop were a school of Spanish refugees, from a relatively comfortable middle class, while the poets linked to Infrarealism came from the working class. But that's all anecdotal, in the end we were all the same, otherwise how could you explain the friendship between Juan Villoro and Roberto, for example? They both came from two very different social classes.

Roberto is a wild writer, his novels are reiterative, he doesn't have a well-planned structure, they're all at a constant peak. He doesn't control their pace, which is why I like the stories much better. As a representative of the second generation of post-boom writing, he injects an enormous amount of energy. Joie de vivre resounds in every phrase, which is why he can't stop. He doesn't edit, he doesn't rewrite, he is incapable of self-criticism. In any case, I think that Bolaño's literary quality isn't something we should be discussing now. What needs to be discussed is the mixture between the character and the person, his relationship with the Latin American medium, which needed to see itself reflected again in a writer. Bolaño appeared when the greats like Neruda, Paz, and Borges had died and the recognition of Vargas Llosa, García Márquez, and Carlos Fuentes had become problematic, controversial, because you agreed with some of the things they said but not others. Roberto was a kind of revelation.

Espinasa places Bolaño in the category of feverish first reads and compares the impact of *The Savage Detectives* with that of *Hopscotch* in its time.

ESPINASA: Can one in their maturity get beyond page one hundred of Julio Cortázar's famous novel? You need to remember how much you loved *Steppenwolf* and yet now you couldn't read it again. There are reads that move us at determined moments of our lifetimes. In Roberto there is a rebel with or without a cause, depending on your point of view. He was committed to the vital act of dedicating twelve long years of agony to a feverish bout of writing that would leave nothing in the inkwell. He was a very intelligent man but I never thought that he would write criticism, and I was proven right. The few works of criticism by him aren't up to the standard of his fiction or poetry, which shows that he wasn't a man to reason about his office. You couldn't ask him to "stop and think about what you're writing" because then he wouldn't write it. Like the Dumas character, if he thought while he walked he would trip over.

The Bolaño of Espinasa's account is an arrogant creature who didn't like to lose arguments, which was why the two often ended up in fistfights. When Bolaño couldn't win, he resorted to invective and was very skilled at goading his opponents.

ESPINASA: There's no doubt that he'd read a lot, but he was surprised to find people who had read the same things he had, with whom he couldn't play teacher. He used this knowledge, all the things he'd read, to gain ascendancy over many of his friends. In his arrogance he tried to revive the Surrealist revolution, when they used to insult Anatole France in the twenties. The equivalent was to turn up at a lecture by Octavio Paz and try to disrupt it by shouting from the audience. The Infras were both childish and fascinating at the same time.

Once we were at the Casa del Lago at a poetry reading and one of the readers was a friend of mine who is now dead too,

Roberto Vallarino, who wrote very solemn poems which weren't at all bad but were very solemn. One of the poems said: "Words name what they name, Roberto is not my name." Then someone from the audience shouted: "No, it's mine." It was Roberto Bolaño. At the time I laughed hard and it seemed a good way to interrupt such a solemn moment. Of course the poet got annoyed, but what can you do.

Just as picking up a guitar at twenty and playing a few chords doesn't make you John Lennon, Espinasa didn't believe that the Infrarealists were writers. To him, the only ones in the group who had any literary quality were Bruno Montané and Roberto Bolaño.

ESPINASA: I liked Mario Santiago a lot but he never seemed a good poet to me. Now that his collected poetry has come out, I feel dutybound as a fellow traveler to write something about it but it won't be a eulogy along the lines of "finally a poet who talks about life," that would be nonsense. One shouldn't be fooled by adolescent fascination. We all want to be young all our lives, to be eternal, but one can be eternal only for two or three years. There's an age at which you can no longer run across the street because your knees ache, and the words ache too, literature also becomes different physically. Not better or worse: just different.

• • •

The Mexican writer Carmen Boullosa met Roberto Bolaño in Mexico in the 1970s, when everyone wanted to be a poet. These were the times when young people led intense literary lives in the cafés, at public readings, going to listen to Octavio Paz talk about Sor Juana Inés de la Cruz. "We were all the same, we dressed in the same way, we were sort of postgraduate hippies, we were like a poetic mass, all very similar," she recalls. "We all thought that we were very elegant but really we all wore sandals and shirts from Oaxaca," she says. "The other band thought that we were bourgeois because we all wore the same thing." According to Boullosa, the friendship developed slowly.

> BOULLOSA: I read the poem by Bolaño that Juan Pascoe published, his first poem, and Pascoe also published a long poem of mine. I first met Bolaño in a group, but I was afraid of the group because they were very poorly behaved: they interrupted poetry readings, heckled people, and started fights. I saw him again twenty years later in Vienna—in around 1998. We were invited to talk about exile, I don't know why I agreed to go. Actually I didn't talk about exile but about how now everyone is a stranger. He didn't talk about exile either, he read a very gentle text about the novel and that was where we became very good friends.

Here is my interview with Boullosa:

> MARISTAIN: *What's the first image of Roberto that pops into your head?*

> BOULLOSA: What a difficult question! The first image of Bolaño that comes is the young Bolaño, the curious Bolaño, the Bolaño from the group of Infrarealist poets, the Oedipal Bolaño who wanted to behead Paz, to get Octavio Paz out of his way. He didn't want a father, he wanted to be his own father. He was an enemy rather than a friend. That's the first Bolaño I think of, the only one who wore ironed clothes, because the rest of us were dirty poets with hemp sandals and a disheveled post-hippie aesthetic. Bolaño, who lived at home with his mother, wore ironed clothes and long hair. He had all the rebelliousness that was part of his personality but there was also a preppy side to him. There

are other Bolaños who are much dearer to me, but they're not the first thing that comes to my mind and I think that that's partly his fault, the fact that he mythologized those youthful years, but partly also because of my memories from the time. Those were formative years for me, when I took shape as a writer and was nourished by a very vibrant, very honest, and very determined literary world.

MARISTAIN: *So you didn't like him?*

BOULLOSA: I was terrified of him and his friends, I didn't like them, I was scared of them. Really, I didn't mind their poems. I liked the long poem that Roberto Bolaño published with Juan Pascoe's Martín Pescador workshop a lot, it was like a bond between the Infras and us, the Pazists. Paz welcomed women writers, while the Efraín Huerta followers had no space for women. I was comfortable where I was and they were on the other side. I was afraid of them because I was very fragile, I was young. When I had to give my first poetry reading as part of the Salvador Novo grant, which Darío Galicia and Verónica Volkow, close friends of Bolaño, had also received, I was very scared because the Infrarealists used to go to those meetings and interrupt them with their heckling. Well, I read in the Gandhi bookshop and they came but didn't interrupt or heckle me.

MARISTAIN: *When did he start to become a nicer Bolaño?*

BOULLOSA: I met Roberto Bolaño again many years later, after he had published *The Savage Detectives*. I had read it, and appreciated how well it depicted my city and generation. I met him in Vienna and we instantly hit it off. We were now writer colleagues and stayed up all night talking. He told me about his children, his wife, and his loves, and I did the same. The two of us almost cried, it was a very intense night. The next day we went for a walk and continued our conversation. I saw him a little later at another writers' event. We used to send each other messages every day; long e-mails. His were longer than mine, mine were sometimes very brief, but Roberto was a fantastic correspondent. Then I went to visit him at home, and I met Carolina. We saw each other in Madrid and Paris. We were close friends up until the day he died. We shared very intimate things with each other and I'd cut off my tongue before I revealed them to anyone [else].

MARISTAIN: *From a literary point of view, how would you describe the Roberto Bolaño phenomenon?*

BOULLOSA: Roberto Bolaño was a very distinctive author who belonged to what I see as a very coherent world. I place him among the great communicating vessels such as José Revueltas, for example, or Octavio Paz, or José Agustín, whom he read very young, and with the great communicating vessels of Anglo-Saxon literature. Roberto was a voracious reader. *2666* is a masterpiece. Then came the fame and the Bolaño phenomenon, which I think has a painful side to it, revealing the cruelty of literature. If Bolaño hadn't died, the phenomenon wouldn't have been so large. The readers and critics who build up literary figures like the concept of an author who dies young, the idea of sacrifice, the romantic death, if you like. The truth is that it upsets me greatly. It upsets me because I knew Roberto, because he was a very dear friend to me and I don't at all like the idea of him being dead, so I can't be comfortable with the culture of cadaver eaters. The other thing that irritates me greatly is when people claim that he wasn't a Latin American author or that he was the only Latin American author. Bolaño is his own father, like any self-respecting author, but he looks better in literary terms next to his peers. So I don't like the cult of death, I don't like the "de-Chileanized" or "de-Mexicanized" Bolaño. If Bolaño had got his liver, he'd still be with us writing wonderful books. Perhaps the acclaim that rings out now that a cadaver, a sacrifice, is involved wouldn't be so loud. I don't like it. And I don't like the way that all this is happening without the author having a right to reply, because he's dead. Bolaño was a professional fighter. By now he'd have fought with who knows how many people, he'd have distanced himself, he'd have set himself apart, he'd have created the confusion that he needed, a shadowy space in which to keep creating. They made him into a statue very quickly.

MARISTAIN: *Who are Bolaño's Latin American peers?*

BOULLOSA: Bolaño is a very literary author, but he doesn't think like Borges, who was an author without an erotic world. Bolaño's literature, in contrast, has very erotic aspects. Also, I think about Bolaño very differently than how I think about Borges. My view is that they have absolutely nothing in common. Some Anglo-Saxon readers have said that Borges and Bolaño are similar, but that's because they haven't read many other Latin American writers. I think that Bolaño's literature is so great because he knew how to create communicating vessels rather than vertical vessels. Vessels that link with their brothers and create dialogues with many other authors. He communicates with César Vallejo, with the Salvadorean poet Roque Dalton: Bolaño's literature is full of literary homages.

MARISTAIN: *Is the strength of his literature felt by only one generation, the youngest generation, or does it have deeper resonance?*

BOULLOSA: I think that people of all generations read.

MARISTAIN: *Is there anything of Bolaño in your literature?*

BOULLOSA: I'm a very different author than Bolaño. I respect him and he respected me, we're from the same generation, we were both educated in Mexico City, but our literatures are very different.

MARISTAIN: *A certain cheekiness and humor, an irony that nonetheless avoids cynicism. There are parallels . . .*

BOULLOSA: I don't know, there's irony in plenty of other books too. To me it's very clear that we're from the same generation, so it was very exciting to read him. When I read *The Savage Detectives* I felt that it was a novel that was very close to me, very much in my territory, but I would never have written something like *The Savage Detectives*. It shows that he came from the school of José Agustín or Efraín Huerta, a less literary world, if you like, although the novel then takes a turn and starts to pursue a writer, which is when it switches sides. To me, it starts out being written by someone affiliated with the Efraín supporters and ends up as if it had fallen under Octavio Paz's influence.

MARISTAIN: *Who is the Bolaño that the Americans are reading at the moment?*

BOULLOSA: I don't know for certain, he's a huge phenomenon there and I think that that's partly because of the sense of sacrifice that comes with the writer dying young. They adore him in the United States. A short while ago I went to an homage to him which drew a big crowd. Jonathan Lethem was there, and he wrote a very important text about Bolaño. The thing is that Bolaño brought something new to the Anglo-Saxons, he came from a tradition that is unfamiliar to them and that's why they tend to compare him to Borges.

MARISTAIN: *Perhaps* The Savage Detectives *changed the way Americans see Latin America ...*

BOULLOSA: That might be true, although I don't fully agree with that notion. Even Gabriel García Márquez, who has created a very diverse world, doesn't always depict a Latin America full of clichés, or rather he doesn't. Neither do I think that there is a single cliché in the United States for Latin America. I don't know what there is but I really don't think that there's a single cliché for Latin America. What there is is deep disdain and huge ignorance. We rank very low in the imperialist mind-set. We're all from a banana republic. Even in the great love for Bolaño I detect a certain disdain because of the way he sacrificed himself, dying young, so they adopted him and took him in. That's also why they built myths around him, ones that make my hair stand on end, saying that he was a heroin addict. Please ...

MARISTAIN: *Now that you've mentioned Jonathan Lethem, what is it that you don't like about his work on Bolaño?*

BOULLOSA: Well, the fact that he places him in the tradition of the Anglo-Saxon authors that both he and Bolaño like. But Lethem is completely different than Bolaño, they have absolutely nothing in common, they have different blood, their genetic message is radically different. They have very slight things in common that he then exaggerates because he doesn't know about the context and so makes Bolaño a kind of Beatnik novelist, which he isn't. What Bolaño really is is a literary animal.

MARISTAIN: *Bolaño is also an uncomfortable figure for established Latin American writers such as Gabriel García Márquez and Carlos Fuentes* ...

BOULLOSA: I think that in his quest to make space for himself it was important to push them off the map, to wipe them out. And I sense that they feel uncomfortable with Bolaño because he didn't pay tribute to them. If Bolaño didn't respect them, why would they respect him? Bolaño is pissing on their territory, like a dog. It's a dogfight over territory.

MARISTAIN: *Do you think that Bolaño is a consummate poet?*

BOULLOSA: No, what I see in Bolaño is a poet working like a mason to build the staircase and foundations for Bolaño the fiction writer. Bolaño the poet interests me greatly. I rescued a book from the public library in New York that I had never read before. It's catastrophically bad, but he is already sketching out the characters in *The Savage Detectives*. That's what he's doing in the poems, drawing studies for his fiction, but he wasn't a complete poet. One day he gave me a book of his poems. I read it and said to him: "Listen, this book's good." And he interrupted me to say: "You know that it's not good, that I'm not a poet. I'm something else."

· · ·

José Vicente Anaya is a poet, essayist, and translator who was born in the north of Chihuahua in 1947. Since 1997, he has run and edited the literary magazine *Alforja* and has become a cultural institution in his own right, a man with a creative instinct and solid principles with roots in the counterculture. He was a young witness to the student uprisings of 1968. His first encounter with Bolaño was dramatic:

ANAYA: I lived in the Condesa neighborhood, in an attic at the top of a building, and every morning, after having breakfast, I would sit down in the center of the apartment, where I had my table, and read, write, or translate. I drank a lot of coffee and left the door ajar. That must have been in 1975. One morning, a fellow with very long hair wearing an overcoat appeared and shouted, "Vicente Anaya!" "Yes," I answered. "I'm a genius!" he replied. It was Roberto Bolaño. I said to him, "I'm a genius, too. Come in," and he sat down to drink some coffee and we started to chat.

During that first shared coffee, Bolaño told Anaya that he had just got back from Chile and was looking for poets who "didn't have anything to do with the status quo," who were rebellious and critical at heart.

"Luis Antonio Gómez, a poet friend of mine, had given him my address and told him to come see me," Anaya said. "The mutual appreciation was immediate. We soon started to go to parties together, leading the fun-loving life that we all enjoyed at the time, although I should point out that I was a little older than Roberto. Every week there was a party somewhere."

It was just a few steps from those parties to the formation of the Infrarealist group. From there, it was just a few days' work to the first manifesto, which established a set of absolute principles.

The poets met to discuss poetry and plan their next move together: publishing a pamphlet featuring poems by the members, trying to place it in the cultural supplements of newspapers, organizing public readings ...

"Thinking about my friendship with Roberto Bolaño, I must acknowledge the many things we agreed on, but also the disputes that arose between he and I right from the beginning," says Anaya.

ANAYA: With regard to the Infrarealist manifesto, I suggested that each member write their own manifesto. My idea was to call for revolt, rebellion, even chaos. If each of us expressed our points of view, if each member of the group showed themselves capable of accepting the others' ideas, even if they didn't agree with them, it would have been interesting. Bolaño flatly opposed my proposal. He said, quite firmly, no, that he was the only one who understood Infrarealism and so he would write the manifesto. The meeting ended without a decision being made, and the truth is that without asking for Bolaño's permission, Mario Santiago and I each wrote a manifesto.

At the end of 1975, three Infrarealist manifestos were written simultaneously: one by Roberto Bolaño, one by Mario Santiago, and one by José Vicente Anaya.

ANAYA: My proposal was to call it Vitalismo. Bolaño's explanation of why he wanted us to call ourselves Infrarealists was very seductive: it referred to science fiction and black holes, transiting infrareal spaces. He convinced us and it was certainly the best name for the group.

La Habana Café, before the Infrarealists turned up, was traditionally frequented, and still is, by journalists working in the newspapers located nearby. Among them at the time was Juan Cervera, who used his journalist's wages to pay for the publication of the anthology of eight Infrarealist poets, *Pájaro de calor* [Bird of Heat].[17]

I'm often asked what happened to the other Infrarealists, Bolaño's companions in the group. I always say that they also published important things. Victor Monjarás-Ruiz, for example, was in my opinion a great chronicler of the twentieth century, he was a filmmaker who made three films, published three notable books of poetry, and he is also a great painter who has had exhibitions in Mexico and France. To me, he is a great artist, although he never received the awards or acclaim that Bolaño did.

José Vicente Anaya explains the success of Roberto Bolaño as being down partly to the discipline he was so proud of and partly to the "lucky break" of the writer deciding to leave for Spain at just the right time. It was easier for him to get his works published there in spite of his difficult beginnings.

"Writers are better treated in Spain, it's much more difficult in Latin America. A great Mexican writer like José Revueltas, for example, is completely unknown outside of this country," says Anaya.

ANAYA: For many years no one talked about the Infrarealists. We were treated with disdain, called intellectual terrorists and bad poets. The success of Roberto Bolaño changed the world of culture's opinion of us. They thought that we hadn't produced any work, but now they know that we have. There are people like Ramón Méndez, for example, who, because of that same inertia on the part of people in power, is still unpublished, though he's written a copious amount of poetry and fiction. I've published thirty books, fifteen of them translated.

A little while ago I saw an interview with Carmen Boullosa on television in New York in which she said that as part of the group that supported Octavio Paz, she and her colleagues made an effort to prevent the publication of the Infrarealists. They apparently used all their influence with publishers to prevent the publication of our work. She says so quite openly, you can see it online. It was true that the group that supported Octavio Paz was very powerful and decided who got literary awards and who got published and who didn't.

The day that Roberto Bolaño said goodbye to me, announcing that he was going to live in Spain, we had an argument. He effectively said: "Now I'm going to go to live in Spain, you can stay and take charge of the world of the Infrarealists, because they're very dispersed and very disorganized." I answered that first I didn't agree that the Infras needed to be "shepherded," because my principles were libertarian and I wasn't going to impose myself on anyone. Second, I didn't take orders from him. Third, I was going to travel too, but around Mexico. I ended by telling him that his authoritarian attitude made him think that he was "the André Breton of the Infras." He answered sardonically: "And you think that you're the Antonin Artaud of the Infras." That was how we parted.

Bolaño and I read together at public readings at the Casa del Lago. A hundred and fifty people came to see us, which was a big crowd for the time. Mara Larrosa, who was very enthusiastic, handed musical instruments out among the audience. So after we had finished reading a poem, we heard noises, applause and shouting. Bolaño and I started to alternate phrases from the Infrarealist manifestos. There was an uproar.

• • •

Hernán Lavín Cerda (born in Santiago de Chile, 1939) is a poet with a long history. He has lived in Mexico since he was forced to go into exile by the Pinochet dictatorship in 1973, and was a privileged witness to the passionate youth of the first, Infrarealist Bolaño with his leadership aspirations. He is one of the eleven poets who appear in *Muchachos desnudos bajo el arcoíris de fuego*, an anthology edited by Bolaño and published in Mexico in 1979.[18]

CERDA: I was thirty-four when I arrived in Mexico. Roberto was in Chile at the time. He came back to Mexico a little after the coup, but he was much younger than me; barely twenty. Yet we had many things in common: admiration for Nicanor Parra, an appreciation of Neruda's poems in *Residencia en la tierra*, plus Jorge Teiller and Enrique Lihn.[19]

What Bolaño did, as I see it, was to bring poetry to the torrent of the novel and it worked for him, although I think that if he had had a choice he would have just written poems his whole life.

He was a very agreeable and ironic young man. He could suddenly come out with a sarcastic quip that you never saw coming. I had plenty of pleasant conversations with him and Mario Santiago, and some others that weren't so pleasant. One day he turned up at the door of my house in Coyoacán together with Bruno Montané. We stood on the threshold and suddenly, with that mischievous smile that was so typical of him, Roberto took some pages out of his backpack and gave them to me. Bruno was standing behind him, looking completely innocent, and not saying anything. He said to me: "Take these, Hernán, I want you to read them and, if you agree, you can sign them." I couldn't believe what I was reading. I said to them: "I'm sorry, but I can't sign this document in these terms because it's a kind of manifesto against UNAM. I came to this country as a political exile, and I've just entered UNAM. Basically, I think that the university respects many different lines of thought, there's a lot of freedom, so ..." Roberto answered me: "I see that the poet 'Ladín' Cerda has become bourgeois." We didn't see each other again.

As a writer, he seems to me a complete writer, with a unique strength and power.

• • •

"I saw Bolaño a couple of times. I met him by chance at La Habana Café," says the poet Francisco Segovia, who was born in Mexico City in 1958 and is now a poet and researcher at El Colegio de México. "I was sitting on my own at a table and he was holding court with a group of other young people. He quoted a few verses to them but couldn't remember the name of the poet. 'Ungaretti,' I said, and he invited me over to the table. I sat talking to him for a while. Bolaño was five years older than me and I occasionally saw him there. On other occasions I saw him through Verónica Volkow and Juan Pascoe, who published our poetry books."

Segovia was on the side of the so-called Pazists together with Carmen Boullosa.

> SEGOVIA: I don't really know how it happened, but Bolaño ended up inviting me to come see him speak. The event was at a house in the Roma neighborhood, on Calle Colima, I think it was the house where Vera and Mara Larrosa lived. It was something of a Bolaño court. I was met by courtiers who took me to the patio. Then they retired and I was left on my own with Bolaño. We had a short conversation in which he told me that I should join his movement. It was like joining a political party led by a pope. I said no. He answered with a phrase that would be the last thing he ever said to me, because I never spoke to him again: "If you're not with me, you're against me."

· · ·

Rodrigo Quijada was born in Chile in 1943. He arrived in Mexico in 1973, fleeing from Augusto Pinochet's military dictatorship. He died in Mexico in 2011. A friend of Poli Délano, a major Chilean author, he was also a poet and writer, and they were occasionally aligned with the Infrarealists.[20] Quijada says that the poets were interested in his and Délano's daughters, and for a short time Roberto Bolaño even dated Bárbara Délano, a poet who died at the age of thirty-five in a plane crash in 1996.

QUIJADA: What I most remember about Bolaño is his enthusiasm, the overwhelming enthusiasm. He was young, spirited, irreverent, and acidic, with a great sense of humor. I think that he was destined to stand out at whatever he put his mind to because of that. Bolaño is the epitome of the young man who gets into literature with the certainty that he is going to triumph. He was free of petulance, conventionalism, pedantry, and at the time he was also a young man in a constant search for love, for promiscuous sexuality …

I met him when he was just twenty years old, but at that age, Roberto already had his path marked out for him, so his success with *The Savage Detectives* wasn't a surprise. I compare him a little to Bukowski; that willingness to explore sordid, dark things, clean them up a little, and then present them to the outside world.

Many literary figures, some critics, especially the Chileans, are unwilling to accept Bolaño. That's envy. There's a saying that if there were a competition for the most envious people in the world, Chile would win first prize. People like Isabel Allende and Antonio Skármeta treat him so disdainfully because they see themselves in competition with him. That's how it is because that's how writers are: despicable. In any case, there aren't many who refuse to see the enormous contribution that Bolaño made to literature, the way he depicted the village in reverse.

He was a fascinating man to whom age didn't matter, he even became close friends with my father. He was willing to talk to anyone so long as he didn't have to make concessions. Bolaño didn't make concessions. That won him unexpected enemies, but the enemies were a result of his frankness, the way he said things that no one wanted to hear or that a lot of people didn't like hearing. Writers are never ready to hear criticism. They always expect compliments, but Bolaño wasn't going to go around handing out compliments.

I don't know if he had many or very few flaws, all I can say is that when I knew him in his youth I didn't see the flaws. Bolaño is one of those people you meet at a certain moment in your life who you will always remember clearly and with great fondness. People who have met Bolaño know what I'm saying is true. He is the kind of man you miss at a gathering. "If only Bolaño were here," we used to say when someone started to get unbearable.

He was a very erudite man who read a lot and knew a lot, but he wasn't the kind of guy who wandered around quoting this or that author to show how much he knew. He wasn't aggressive. I never saw him in a violent situation. His arguments were fiery but poetic, and in the end we all agreed with him on the basic points. It was a great privilege to know him and not because he later became famous. He was one of those people you meet and who makes an important impression on you.[21]

6

Scribblers

Confusing the hit parade with literature—Light-years be-tween one and the other—The curse of legibility—The writer's torments—Hand over fist—A mistake I will pay for for the rest of my life—They're beyond even God's help—If you don't understand the allusions—Strangeness—My children are my homeland

Roberto Bolaño's mordant, provocative wit coined the term *escribidora* (scribbler). It was mainly to describe his compatriot Isabel Allende, who, in an interview published in *El País* in September 2003, answered to the term with great annoyance: "It didn't bother me, because he bad-mouthed everyone. He never had a good word for anyone. The fact that he's dead doesn't, in my opinion, make him a better writer. He was a very unpleasant person."

Bolaño first used the term in a telephone interview with the Chilean journalist Andrés Gómez on May 26, 2002, for *La Tercera*. Asked about the candidates that year for the National Award for Literature in his home country, for which Allende was the favorite, Bolaño answered: "I think that she is a bad writer, plain and simple. To call her a writer is to do her too much credit. I don't even think Isabel Allende is a writer, she's an *escribidora*." Of course, the fact that the author of *The House of the Spirits* sold so many copies of her books wasn't, to Bolaño, an argument to be taken into consideration: "In that case we'll have to give the Pulitzer to John Grisham or Ken Follet. That would be to confuse the hit parade with literature. They have nothing to do with each other."

Referring to the category of *escribidora* in which Allende was placed, the Argentine critic Mónica López Ocón wrote in the magazine *Ñ*, the cultural supplement of the newspaper *Clarín*: "Roberto Bolaño said that Isabel Allende isn't a writer but an 'escribidora.' If this term is understood as a kind of fictional bureaucracy where formulas are repeated, and the writing is flat and serves an ideological-marketing objective in which womanhood is converted into a stereotype of heroism, then Bolaño was right."[1]

Bolaño himself explained the difference between a writer and an *escribidora*: "Silvina Ocampo is a writer. Marcela Serrano is an *escribidora*. There are light-years between them."

In an interview, Felipe Ríos Baeza, a young Chilean professor from the Universidad de Puebla, expands this idea further.

RÍOS BAEZA: Any reader with a passing knowledge of Roberto Bolaño's work can see a fundamental aspect of it: his great ethical and aesthetic sense of the office of writing. Ethical because on several occasions he said that any contact with political and economic power makes an apprentice writer into a courtesan. Aesthetic, because he argued that legibility—the books you take to the beach, books that are easy to understand and have no critical or artistic depth—was something that helped to finance publishers but offered little critical meaning to readers. Very perceptive people have written about this, including Pierre Bourdieu (*The Rules of Art*) and Enrique Vila-Matas (*Aunque no entendamos nada* [Even Though We Don't Understand Anything]), but for starters you can read "The Myths of Cthulhu" or "The Vagaries of the Literature of Doom" by Bolaño himself.

In summary, readability and prostitution produce hacks, simple receptacles for conventional techniques and subjects with which publishers attract mass readerships to the "new releases" table. A scribbler is someone who doesn't take aesthetic risks, they repeat well-worn narrative tropes (paperbacks in which the woman is oppressed by a patriarchy or that recycle the regional folklore of a Latin America devastated by the United Fruit Company) and generally are interested only in boiling a story down without understanding that literature, like any artistic discipline, should have different aesthetic and epistemological levels.

In a June 2005 interview with the Argentine journalist Eliseo Álvarez, published in the magazine *Turia*, Bolaño referred once more to Allende and Serrano: "If I had grown up with my mother's tastes, right now I'd be a kind of Marcela Serrano or Isabel Allende. It wouldn't be that bad because I wouldn't have known the torment of being a writer and would have earned money hand over fist, which, thinking about it, wouldn't be such a bad thing."

Over time the term *escribidora* came to describe an aesthetic typified not only by Allende but also writers such as Ángeles Mastretta, Antonio Skármeta, and the Spanish writer Arturo Pérez Reverte.

Bolaño's readers understand perfectly the meaning and application of the term *escribidora*, which may also unwittingly define a type of reader as decisively as Julio Cortázar's distinction between "Reader/feminine (passive) and Reader/masculine (active)."

Bolaño had already been involved in an earlier dispute with Mastretta in 1999, when he won the Rómulo Gallegos Prize for *The Savage Detectives*. In his famous speech in Caracas, he said: "... and I'd like to take advantage of these parentheses to thank the jury for this honor, especially Ángeles Mastretta ..." The author of *Arráncame la vida* (Take My Life Away) was the only member of the jury who voted against Bolaño in favor of *Caracol Beach*, by the Cuban writer Eliseo Alberto.[2]

In an interview published on November 16, 2008, in the *C* Sunday supplement of the now defunct newspaper *Crítica* in Argentina, Ángeles Mastretta mentioned the episode.

MASTRETTA: Not voting for *The Savage Detectives* was a mistake that I have paid for ever since. It's great that I now have the chance to say that, because no one has ever asked me about it before. Yes, I voted against Bolaño and I was very wrong. It's true that I liked the novel by Eliseo Alberto, *Caracol Beach*, much better, or at least I understood it much better, but now that Bolaño is a cult author and I've been able to decipher him little by little I'd say that I respect him even though his literature isn't the kind that excites me. That afternoon I lost my integrity, I'll never vote against a whole jury again. The truth is that not many of Bolaño's fans like me but I'm not going to let it bother me. It's more important that I now understand who Bolaño is and that I've become a fan of his.

Bolaño also seemed to have personal issues with Antonio Skármeta, the author of *Ardiente paciencia* (Burning Patience) and *Soñé que la nieve ardía* (I Dreamed That the Snow Was on Fire), among other works. In an interview with Andrés Gómez for *La Tercera*, Bolaño said: "Skármeta is a TV personality. I can't read a single book of his, flicking through his prose turns my stomach. I mean: Allende's literature is bad, but it's alive. You can't say that about Skármeta or Teitelboim. They're beyond even God's help."[3]

The criticisms of Isabel Allende—who eventually won the Chilean National Prize for Literature in 2010—and Skármeta are a pale reflection of the very prickly relationship the author of *2666* had with Chilean literature in general, an attitude that has certainly been detrimental to his standing among his compatriots, many of whom, like Skármeta himself, want nothing to do with him.

In an unpublished interview in Zacatecas in 2010, part of the Hay Literatura festival, Skármeta declined to speak about Bolaño and defensively said that "talking about these things causes controversy and I don't want to cause controversy."

In several interviews, when he is called to assess new Latin American literature, Skármeta—like his Nicaraguan colleague and friend Sergio Ramírez—describes the Dominican Junot Díaz as a "must read."

When an Argentine literature professor asked him at a congress in Brazil to explain his opinion of the relationship between Junot Díaz and Bolaño, Skármeta said, "If you don't understand the allusions ..."

The author of *The Brief Wondrous Life of Oscar Wao* is amused by the comparison: "My two little books are more important than Roberto Bolaño's life's work? That's the most ridiculous thing I've heard this year, and in New York I hear ridiculous things every day."

Díaz sees it this way: "These things happen because in Latin America there are too many macho writers who don't understand that reading someone isn't the same as being friends with them. I see literature as a strategy, and no one can deny or reject a strategy. Also, writing is so difficult that I don't want to reject my enemies, you never know when someone else's book is going to save your own writing."[4]

Bolaño himself seems to acknowledge the concept of the macho writer in the Latin American canon, although his definition contrasts with the Cortázarian one. In a piece praising the Peruvian Jaime Bayly, he says: "What a relief it is to read Bayly's literature after an interminable succession of talentless Latin American *machitos*, snobs of shackled prose, loudmouthed bureaucratic heroes of the proletariat."

Sergio Ramírez, in an interview with the journalist Silvina Friera for the Argentine newspaper *Página/12* published on October 30, 2010, says, referring especially to Bolaño: "For the new generations the first great writer was Borges—i.e., not García Márquez—and his representative on earth was Bolaño. That generation hasn't been able to find a literary voice of its own. One might say that Bolaño is the great rebel but that's not enough to define a path. That's not a criticism, just natural, because it's still very early to say how the new generation will develop, how the new Latin American literature will be written."

So was Bolaño right when he said he was the writer with
the longest past and the shortest future of anyone? Apart from
personal appreciations and tastes, it is rather ungenerous if not
downright mean to deny the influence of work as profuse as Bolaño's. Literature isn't, or shouldn't be, about what is going to
happen, but about what is written, what can actually be read. One
can perhaps read between the lines of the negative assessments
to see the animosity that an agitator like Bolaño created among
the post-boom authors who don't hold the Chilean author in
high esteem.

Harold Bloom says that it is "strangeness" that makes an author and their work canonical, "a form of originality that either
cannot be assimilated or that assimilates us so that we no longer
see it as strange."

In his prologue to the book *Roberto Bolaño: Ruptura y violen-
cia en la literatura finisecular* (Roberto Bolaño: Rupture and Violence in Literature at the End of the Century), a volume of
twenty-one critical essays gathered by the Universidad de Puebla,
Felipe Ríos Baeza says: "Next to figures such as Enrique Vila-
Matas and Martin Amis, Michel Houellebecq and J. M. Coetzee,
the post-boom had little to offer in either form or substance.
Until the end of the twentieth century, a Latin American writer
had an all-conquering idea: to delve into the Western canon,
ransack it of its forms and styles, and write a novel that was both
a dictionary and a biographical record. In the same tradition as
La sinagoga de los iconoclastas [The Synagogue of Iconoclasts] by
Juan Rodolfo Wilcock, *Historia universal de la infamia* [A Universal History of Infamy] by Jorge Luis Borges, and even *Vidas
imaginarias* [Imaginary Lives] by Marcel Schwob, Seix Barral[5]
published *Nazi Literature in the Americas* by the then unknown
Roberto Bolaño in 1996."

Jorge Volpi is the Mexican author of *En busca de Klingsor* (In
Search of Klingsor). In *Mentiras contagiosas* (Contagious Lies),

in which Volpi announces the end of Latin American literature, he explains the reluctance of the literary establishment to give Bolaño a place in the canon next to Carlos Fuentes, Gabriel García Márquez, Mario Vargas Llosa, and Julio Cortázar: "Look for a writer under forty (you'll no doubt be able to find one in the bar on the corner) and ask them about Bolaño: more than 80 percent, without exaggeration, will say that he's the daddy, that he's the dude; wonderful, great, fantastic. Then ask a writer older than forty (you'll find them in the bar across the street, or a ministry, or a retirement home) and you'll find that 80 percent of the time they have one, several, or lots of misgivings."

In the year 2000, during the launch of a book of poems by Carlos Fuentes Lemus (Carlos Fuentes's eldest son, who died in 1999), journalists asked the author of *Aura* what he thought of Roberto Bolaño, who had just won the Rómulo Gallegos, a prize he himself had won in 1977 for *Terra Nostra*. The Mexican answered with a curt, serious phrase: "I don't know him."

On August 27, 2011, Fuentes published an article in *El País*, an extract from his forthcoming book *The Great Latin American Novel*. In that text, the writer ignores Bolaño entirely, omitting him from his list of the most important authors of the twenty-first century.

On April 13, 2009, in an interview with Radio Cooperativa in Santiago de Chile, Fuentes said that he'd wait a few years to read Bolaño: "I haven't read him yet because I sense that a sort of funerary homage still lingers around him. I don't like that so I'll wait a few years before reading him seriously. As a living writer.

"I feel that I can't get close to him because of all the noise around him, I can still see the funeral wreaths everywhere, I can't avoid them and I'd rather see Bolaño as a living writer," he repeated.

The Peruvian Mario Vargas Llosa had a different reaction. In 2008, he said to a television journalist: "A few books by a Chilean writer, Bolaños [*sic*], a wonderful writer, have just come out. I recommend all his books, but mainly the novel *The Savage Detectives*."

In 2010, he went further in a conversation on Italian television:

VARGAS LLOSA: There were pessimists who said that literature in Spanish had come to the end of an era, that it was in decline and that it was no longer of interest outside Spanish-speaking countries. Of course, the myth that now surrounds him helped, the one created by his dramatic life, his early death, those last years on his deathbed, writing with one foot in the grave, all that created a myth ... but the myth has in this respect served to help garner recognition for an original body of work, one of real quality. The people who knew Bolaño know that he was different from the public Bolaño of today, the international figure created by the critics, by his readers and by the legend that sprang up around him. One can understand why they sometimes say: "No, they're wrong, he wasn't like that, that's not it ..." But whether they're right or wrong, a figure is produced not just by the events of a person's life but also the images, the fantasies, that the books that person wrote conjure for his readers and critics. When he wrote criticisms he was very patricidal, he criticized previous generations very harshly, which is always healthy. The only way for children to free themselves and achieve their own voice is by killing their parents; it was a ritual that he fulfilled very diligently.

At the same time, it can't be said that [Bolaño] wasn't generous, because there were writers from previous generations about whom he was very enthusiastic. Borges, for example: he wrote a lot of brilliant things about him ... When I started to read *Nazi Literature in the Americas*, I realized that it was a fake, a fictional book playing a slightly Borgesian game of inventing authors, books, commenting on them and through the commentary on these books which he himself invented, putting together a fictional story. It was a very intelligent, brilliant, original book, full of ideas and irony. Furthermore, I thought that *The Savage Detectives* was a great novel; ambitious, with a wonderful beginning especially. I think that those first hundred pages describing the world of bohemian Mexico, almost an underworld, are wonderfully well done. Then the novel takes a sharp turn and becomes a game. His life [Bolaño's] was an adventure, his life was a novel with a tragic end, the premature, young death and the desperation of the last years of writing, writing, literature as a kind of life raft for a drowning man ... Well, all that has contributed to the Bolaño myth, which I also think is in his literature, giving his literature its great vitality and dynamism.

So was Bolaño an irrepressible, irresistible provocateur? And if so, why? And of what? According to the poet Rubén Medina, one of the founders of the Infrarealist movement, Bolaño's formative poetical attitude was "a form of approaching the abyss in a way that writers don't tend to, a form of exploring, of writing poetry, a way to screw with your fellow man."

And then there was Chilean literature, a body of work that aroused deep-seated passions in Bolaño. It was a sphere in which he chose a role for himself as a pitiless critic, as in his final interview, when he offered up a summary of what Chilean literature was.

BOLAÑO: Probably the nightmares of the most rancorous, gray, and perhaps the most cowardly of the Chilean poets: Carlos Pezoa Véliz, who died at the start of the twentieth century and only wrote two memorable poems, although they were truly memorable and still keep us dreaming and suffering. It's possible that Pezoa Véliz hasn't yet died, that he's still on his deathbed and his final minute is taking an age, don't you think? And we're all experiencing it with him. Or at least all Chileans are.

Jorge Volpi, in an interview published by *El Mercurio* on September 18, 2010, says: "Bolaño went back to Chile like a bull in a china shop, and nurtured by distance and accumulated resentment, he exploded onto the literary scene with a bang, throwing out gibes and punches left and right. I witnessed his two faces myself: his good, quite sweet nature in private and his almost offensive stridency in public."

The Argentine scholar Valeria Bril pushes this idea further in an article titled "Bolaño: A Man Lost in Chilean Literature."

BRIL: The "imaginative landscape" of Chilean literature oppressed Roberto Bolaño because it avoided the great themes of literature. From his point of view, Chilean literature had forgotten the narratives full of utopian, all-encompassing discourse from the sixties and had succumbed to a generation of more individualistic writers less committed to a literary tradition. Roberto Bolaño's idea of literature, especially Chilean literature, can be summed up in these words: "Literature, as I suppose I've made clear, has nothing to do with national awards but a strange shower of blood, sweat, semen, and tears. Especially sweat and tears … I don't know what Chilean literature has to do with any of that. Neither, frankly, do I care."

In a country that gave the National Literature Prize to Gabriel Mistral in 1951 when the author had already won the Nobel in 1945, it is significant that Bolaño described the literary forces of his homeland with the phrase "season in hell." He wrote: "Don't fight because you will always be defeated … Don't be stinting with your praise for idiots, the dogmatic, the mediocre, if you don't want to live in a season in hell."[6] (In another mark of Bolaño's dissatisfaction with the literary culture of his home country, he once wrote that Chileans go to literary events in the same mood as they visit their psychiatrist.)[7]

Notoriously, Roberto Bolaño never won the National Prize for Literature in Chile, not even posthumously. Referring to the award, the Chilean writer and journalist Rolando Gabrielli, who now lives in Panama, says: "The Chilean National Prize for Literature has a corrosive effect on national literature. It was founded seventy-eight years ago as a national fund to lift writers with no other means of support out of poverty. In spite of its pompous claim to be the leading award, it has nonetheless become an ideal arena for snubbing, cutting people down to size, and airing one's dirty laundry in public for the winners, the losers, and the eternal candidates, all this presided over by a government bureaucrat."[8]

The only prize that Bolaño won in Chile was the Municipal Prize of Santiago for his book *Phone Calls*. (A selection of stories from *Putas Aseinas* [2001] and *Llamadas Telefónicas* [Phone Calls] [1997] was published in English in April 2007 as *Last Evenings on Earth*.) The jury was chaired by the writer and diplomat Roberto Ampuero.

"I followed Roberto Bolaño with great interest from the start," remembers Ampuero. "I always thought that he wasn't treated as he should have and deserved to be treated in Chile. I even at one time joined the calls for him and Isabel Allende to be awarded the National Prize for Literature. I only spoke to him once, on the telephone, to tell him that he had won the Municipal Prize. He was incredulous."

Not surprising, as Bolaño was a man who specifically felt that the only homeland he belonged to was one rooted in his children, his son and daughter: Lautaro, born in 1990, and Alexandra, born in 2001.

"My children are my homeland," he once said. Chile was never mentioned.

7

Two Dissidents and a Lonely Gaucho

Anticanonical Latin American novels—Bolaño's perspective is like Witold Gombrowicz's perspective—We'll see each other soon, here or anywhere else

Given our ever-increasing life expectancies, which promise future generations thousand-year lives, one must accept that Roberto Bolaño didn't just die young, but very young, when he was barely out of adolescence.

One must also recognize that his was a pubescent personality in the sacrosanct literary universe whose norms he wiped out with the strokes of his pen. When there is discussion of long-lived authors, José Saramago's name always comes up. He published his first important novel, *Baltasar and Blimunda*, in 1982, when he was sixty, taking his career to another level and eventually receiving the Nobel Prize before he died at the age of eighty-seven.

The critic Ignacio Echevarría says, "If Bolaño had been able to experience the prominence that he was achieving, I think that he would have exaggerated or faked his tendency to be mischievous."

Who knows how Bolaño's relationships with his colleagues would have developed if it weren't for his early death. The famous canon, often the object of his unbound fury, his arbitrary tendency to raise or lower his thumb according to his stronger or weaker sympathies, and his voracious, anti-academic reading, which was nonetheless varied enough to give him a wide-ranging view of the contemporary literary spectrum, would have undergone numerous transformations.

In 2001, the *Babelia* supplement in *El País* was good enough to unite two "dissidents" from the canon of the Latin American boom: the Chilean Roberto Bolaño and the Argentine Ricardo Piglia.

They exchanged e-mails, which were later published in *Babelia*. During the virtual conversation, both authors explored, among other issues, the concept of "Latin Americanness" as applied to their works and those that preceded them.

In Argentine literature, a territory over which Jorge Luis Borges casts a gigantic shadow, Ricardo Piglia, born in Buenos Aires in 1941, is one of the paradigmatic narrators of the new era, able to address that shadow on equal terms. He is an inescapable point of reference in trying to understand some of the enigmas of the dense, powerful fiction that comes out of Argentina. With his literary work—his most notable book being *Artificial Respiration*, published in 1980 when the Argentine dictatorship that was formed after the 1976 coup d'état governed with a bloody, iron fist—the author shone a powerful spotlight on his surroundings, building firm lines of communication with a tradition to which he is luxuriously indebted, with a characteristically visionary perspective. He is a universal writer who can be enjoyed by readers with very different backgrounds.

His novels, stories (he first came to prominence in 1967 when his first story collection, *La invasión* [The Invasion], won the Casa de las Américas award), and nonfiction have made this tenacious, incredibly consistent writer one of the most complex and fascinating authors in the contemporary literary universe. His baroque but sharp critical quill has been turned to Roberto Arlt, Jorge Luis Borges, Macedonio Fernández, and Manuel Puig, and together they make up a range of influences whose sense of experimentation and unimpeachable intellectual rigor have enhanced his powerful literary voice.

Together with another great Argentine writer, Juan José Saer (1937–2005), Piglia is a leading light in a tradition that provides an alternative to the boom led by Gabriel García Márquez. This tradition presented a creative dissidence that was most fruitful when acting in parallel to the magical realism that attracted all the attention in the 1970s. It was a path expressed in a different literary register, but one just as fertile as the one that created established, widely read works such as *One Hundred Years of Solitude*. It is currently being reevaluated with the zeal of one discovering something that was always there. This register replaces the unbridled fantasy of magical realism with a grotesque, provocative surrealism that disrespectfully but very cleverly parodies diffuse concepts such as "the Argentine" and the oft-discussed Latin American reality.

"It seems to me that new constellations are forming, the ones that we can see from our laboratory when we point our telescope at the night sky," Piglia said to Bolaño.

As an inhabitant of this flamboyant constellation, Ricardo Piglia describes himself as being part of the same humble but aristocratic circles that Borges mixed with in his time. "Sometimes I think that I'm read only by a group of friends, and that, to me, is success," he says with convincing sweetness.

Perhaps overwhelmed by the success of *Blanco nocturno*, his first novel in thirteen years (in 1997, he published *Platt quemada* [Money to Burn], which was later made into a successful film), which made him the center of attention not only in his country but also across Latin America and Spain, he subsequently announced that he was only going to write stories from then on: "If the publishing market doesn't want stories, then we have to write them," he said.[1]

Ricardo Piglia's novel is a crime story that takes place in an oppressive village atmosphere, where everyone knows everyone else and their past, and Officer Croce and his assistant investigate the murder of a Puerto Rican visitor. As the story goes on, the book wittily parodies the gaucho tradition of Argentina, which, according to Piglia, "owes its existence to memories that create an ideal touristy vision of the country."

Regarding the influences on *Blanco nocturno*, which explores

themes such as the relationship between the city and the countryside, the Argentine author mentions William Faulkner as his
principal source of inspiration.

"He was the one who built Yoknapatawpha County, the
imaginary place that was later repeated in the Macondo of Gabriel García Márquez and the Comala of Juan Rulfo, among
others," he says.

Piglia mentions one of Borges's anecdotes about Macedonio
Fernández, who would jokingly say: "The gauchos were invented
to entertain the horses in their stables." This amusement toward
the pompous solemnity of a conservative folklore that seeks, in
vain, to dominate the culture of an entire country provides the
meat of Piglia's book, and endears him still further to the new
generations of readers who venerate him.

It is impossible not to relate the anticanonical attitude, expressed not as a mockery of the traditional landscape of a literature trapped in its own anachronistic myths but as a way of
seeing the same landscape with new eyes, with the masterful
story "The Insufferable Gaucho" (dedicated by the author to his
Argentine friend and colleague Rodrigo Fresán), which appeared
in the eponymous story collection that Bolaño prepared before
his death. In it, "the gauchos had sold their horses to the slaugh-
terhouse, and now got around on foot, or on bicycles, or hitched
rides on the endless dirt tracks of the pampas."[2]

"Buenos Aires is rotten, I'm going to the ranch," says Héctor
Pereda before moving to a untamed land where horses are now
useless, the celebrated Argentine beef is replaced by wild rabbits
cooked in every way possible, and where, in the taverns, otherwise
known as "smoking churches," the customers play Monopoly.

Bolaño would seem to be an expert on the subject, as can be
seen in the speech "The Vagaries of the Literature of Doom,"
dedicated to another Argentine writer, Alan Pauls, and pub-

lished posthumously in *Between Parentheses*. "If *Martín Fierro* dominates Argentine literature and its place is in the center of the canon, the work of Borges, probably the greatest writer born in Latin America, is only a footnote," he said.[3]

Several years later, the Mexican writer Álvaro Enrigue would come out with another anticanonical novel, *Decencia* (Decency), which in a similar manner attacks the icons of Mexico. Enrigue even sticks it to tequila, the national drink par excellence, which, through the false virtues of brown sugar and sweetener, conceals the wild idiosyncrasy of a tough, savage country that suffers and makes others suffer in turn.

Like Ricardo Piglia in *Blanco nocturno*, especially when the Argentine author says that the gauchos didn't really eat meat, because they didn't have any teeth, Enrigue tears apart the patriotic myths and folklore of his country, mercilessly leaving it as bare as the most featureless desert.

"Whatever the intellectuals of kitsch who have taken this country over, a country that was once proud of the anger of its people, say, there's nothing less memorable than a childhood spent in the provinces. All praise of the province eventually becomes a sardonic comment on boredom," says Enrigue.

In the virtual conversation between Piglia and Bolaño, they discuss the issue of translators, whom the Argentine calls "the real damned writers," and the Chilean's insightful interest in "four key reference points" in Argentine literature: Macedonio Fernández, Jorge Luis Borges, Roberto Arlt, and Witold Gombrowicz. The latter, of course, was a Pole who accidentally ended up living in Argentina. As Malcom Lowry did in Mexico with *Under the Volcano*, Gombrowicz helped stitch together the patchwork of the national identity of a people trapped in its own sorry folklore (as the case with Mexico) or by seductive pressure from abroad (as with Argentina).

They also mention an Argentine who later became an Italian citizen, Juan Rodolfo Wilcock, to whom Bolaño was particularly devoted, and, of course, Manuel Puig, the author of *Kiss of the Spider Woman*, who, like Lowry, also lived for a time in Cuernavaca, Mexico.

These were authors who, like Bolaño, were, intentionally or otherwise, estranged geographically, but who weren't content to inhabit apocryphal spaces. They rather sought to give meaning to every place they set foot in.

In fact, at the inauguration of the Bolaño Course initiated by the Diego Portales University in Santiago de Chile in 2010, Ricardo Piglia linked Gombrowicz to Bolaño.

PIGLIA: I'd like to remember Roberto Bolaño—with whom I had very intense and fun conversations—and point out that the title of this talk, "The Writer as Reader," could also very well be a way to define Bolaño's perspective and work.

The selected theme, linked to certain experiences of the Polish writer Witold Gombrowicz, would, I think, also have pleased Bolaño. He once said—with his ever-so-productive irony and sarcasm—that if instead of expending so much energy on Roberto Arlt, I had focused on Witold Gombrowicz, things would have been different. I always asked him: "What things would have been different?" So, trying to assess what some of those different things might have been, I thought it might be appropriate, in memory of Bolaño, to speak about Gombrowicz. It seems to me that there is a relationship between Gombrowicz's and Bolaño's perspectives.

What we're calling here "the perspective" of a writer is their poetics: the way in which a writer reads, sees the world, and everything else. So one can talk about Bolaño's and Gombrowicz's gaze as, in a sense, a synchronous movement.

What I'm trying to say is that there are always traces of what a writer reads in their work. And in the work of Bolaño, the presence of fictionalized readings in his texts makes him one of the most important writers in any language: the way in which he has made reading into an adventure, often featuring intrigue, pursuits, and quests.

Piglia and Bolaño also talked about friendship, which the Chilean contrasts with love, saying that lovers can accept certain levels of contemptibility that would be unthinkable between friends.

The conversation concludes with an affectionate Piglia inviting his counterpart to be a friend beyond literature. "Come to see me in California whenever you want, I'll be going to Barcelona soon, where I hope to see you," says Piglia.

Bolaño answers: "I hope we'll see each other soon, here or anywhere else."

8

A Real Son of Parra

Antipoetry is pure poetry—The booksellers—The ghost of Santiago de Chile—The author of Las Cruces

Although the Chilean stand at the twenty-fifth Guadalajara International Book Fair, in 2011, had only a small, modest edition of *Poems and Antipoems* at the ridiculous price of twenty-five dollars, the literary world gathered at the fair joyfully celebrated the award of the Cervantes Prize to the Chilean poet Nicanor Parra.

Antonio Skármeta, author of *The Postman*, exultantly pointed to the good wine produced by Chile as an explanation for "the strength of our literature."

"He's an idol for many young people. The youngest, the ones who are still thin and have all their own hair, love him too. Parra's words are immediately discussed as soon as they are pronounced. Whatever he says has a profound affect ... If you push the Parra key, the true essence of Chile appears," added Skármeta.

The Argentine bookseller Natu Poblet, owner of the legendary Clásica y Moderna bookshop, celebrated the major award given to the ninety-six-year-old poet, "because it's finally been given to someone from South America and because ... Nicanor [was an icon] of freedom for Argentinians when we were suffering from the cruel years of the dictatorship."

The Mexican writer Alberto Ruy-Sánchez said, "Since I was a teenager, Nicanor Parra has to me meant antisolemnity, not just in poetry but also as a way of living. I'm very happy."

"I'm very glad that they've given the Cervantes to Nicanor Parra," the Spanish writer Almudena Grandes said. "I think that it's a very fair choice. He has been a candidate for many years. And whenever an older writer who has waited for a prize for a long time is given it, it's a reason to celebrate."

The Mexican writer Jorge Volpi, one of the best students of Latin American literature, expressed his overwhelming joy "over a very well-deserved prize. In 1991, Nicanor came to Mexico to receive the Juan Rulfo Prize. All those years passed and now he's won the Cervantes. He deserved it long before," he said.

"Anyone with the good fortune to come across the work of Nicanor Parra will find a poet who can charm the reader," said the Mexican author Alberto Chimal, "because he is like a rock, like a mountain. There are light poets who never touch the ground. Parra, in contrast, is rooted to the ground, his work is unavoidable. In fact, I'm surprised that he hasn't won the Cervantes Prize before."

"What Nicanor Parra's work has is great coherence that can explode whatever went before, breaking with established patterns," said the writer Juan Sasturáin. "He burst onto the Chilean poetry scene, which isn't just any scene, with a voice that was completely different than Vicente Huidobro, Pablo Neruda, and Gonzalo Rojas, and that makes him a genuine literary giant."

His compatriot, the poet Diana Bellessi, was pleased. "We must celebrate every time a poet is given an award. I've enjoyed his poetry very much for the thirty years since the majority of his work was published," she declared.

None of them mentioned what Roberto Bolaño, who might be seen as the true heir to Nicanor Parra, pointed out in an article dedicated to the illustrious Chilean poet, who, because of his age, sent his grandson to receive the Cervantes Prize, carrying an old typewriter on which he had written (displaying what Ignacio Echevarría might call "another Parrian act of mischievousness"):

Did you expect this prize?
No.

Prizes are like Dulcinea of Toboso + we think of them + from
afar + deaf to us + enigmatic
Prizes are for free spirits for friends of the jury
Really. You didn't expect me to be so cunning.

In an article titled "Eight Seconds for Nicanor Parra," which
accompanied an exhibition on Parra in Madrid in 2001, Roberto
Bolaño referred to the lasting nature of the antipoet's work. This
was especially significant praise when one considers that Bolaño
hated the concept of immortality as applied to art.

"If you have the merest idea of literature, how many Latin
American writers from the decade between 1870 and 1880 are still
relevant today? In a thousand years, even Shakespeare will be
forgotten," Roberto said to the journalist Cristián Warnken.

"There's only one thing I can say for sure about Nicanor
Parra's poetry in this new century: it will endure," Bolaño wrote
in the catalog.[1] "This means very little, of course, as Parra would
be the first to acknowledge it. Still, it will endure, along with the
poetry of Borges, Vallejo, Cernuda, and a few others. But this, it
must be said, hardly matters."

At the age of nineteen, Roberto Bolaño picked up a copy of
Artefactos by Nicanor Parra in a bookshop in Santiago. It was 1972
and Bolaño had returned to his country after a long journey over
land and sea. While he was there, he was caught up in Augusto
Pinochet's bloody coup, which deposed Salvador Allende. As he
remembered it, he was one of the few people in the bookstores
during Chile's time of unrest.

Bolaño was never reluctant to say that Parra was his poetic
touchstone, his favorite bard. "Nicanor Parra's antipoetic manifesto is the purest kind of poetry," said Bolaño. Bolaño's colleague
and friend Bruno Montané described Bolaño's poetry writing
as a means of "entering the tremulous passage of life through

writing ... he'd perhaps rather have been Nicanor Parra decipher-
ing the monologues of Leopoldo María Panero in a single fleet-
ing visit to his house at Las Cruces."

Nicanor Parra and Roberto Bolaño met in 1998 during a now
famous visit that Bolaño made to him on the coast at Las Cruces, where Parra still lives.

In an article Bolaño later wrote about the visit, he admitted to
being nervous; he was, after all, going to meet "the great man," the
most lucid poet of his generation, the author of *Poems and Antipoems*.[2] Ignacio Echevarría, who witnessed the encounter, told the
story at a conference at Diego Portales University in Santiago de
Chile. He also shared his impressions of the relationship in an
interview: "I think that, as often happens with great talents, Parra
and Bolaño somehow recognized each other at first sight. And
Bolaño, who had admired Parra from long before, then put him
at the center of his constellation of literary saints."[3]

Echevarría sees antipoetry as a "decisive influence" on Bolaño. "Especially with regard to how to direct a literary vocation characterized by the rejection of the establishment, a certain
kind of integrity, and the search for a new, radical way to understand literature."

After the visit to Las Cruces, Echevarría, with Roberto's en-
couragement, and together with Niall Binns, the English expert
in Hispanic literature, took charge of the publication of the *Complete Works* of Nicanor Parra. The book was published in Spanish
as a two-volume work, 2,229 pages in total. Nicanor, who was reluctant at first, decided to publish it because it was "what Roberto would have wanted," says Echevarría.[4]

Bolaño's son, Lautaro, understands this affinity with Nicanor
as well.

LAUTARO BOLAÑO: I now remember Nicanor Parra's grandson
in a very pretty house with palm trees, on the coast, I think. The

grandson was teasing me, saying: "I'm Lautara and I want to be your girlfriend." I remember that I discovered those bags, I don't know what they're called, they're made of plastic and you can seal them. ["A hot water bottle?"] Yes, I'd never seen one of them in my life. I asked Nicanor's grandson to show it to me but he said: "Only if you show me how to play chess." My father taught me how to play chess when I was eight or nine. He said to me: "I'll beat you in three moves." I didn't believe him, but he did in fact beat me in three moves with his strategies.[5]

9

Roberto Did Very Strange Things

*Anecdotes from a dark Barcelona—A sponge of a guy—
What the hell do women want?—Coffee, fried eggs, and
spaghetti—Let's go out for coffee, it's cold in here*

Jaime Rivera moves his arms when he speaks. It looks as though he's dancing. He's over sixty but all his energy is condensed into almost adolescent gestures, as if he were standing at the entrance to a club, trying to invite everyone passing by to the party.

It's a Saturday on the Rambla in Barcelona, and the Chilean artist is selling his work at one of the stalls. Next to him, his ex-wife and the mother of his child is selling colorful shirts.

Together with the poet Bruno Montané, Jaime was one of Roberto's closest friends in the first stage of the writer's life in Barcelona. Rivera was also very close to Bolaño's mother, Victoria Ávalos; he was practically part of the family.

Rivera studied art at the Faculty of Fine Art in Santiago de Chile. He was adjunct professor of painting at the School of Fine Arts in the Chilean capital until he had to leave his home country in 1974 "at the request" of Pinochet's military junta. Since then, he has lived and worked in Barcelona.

He met Roberto in the dark Barcelona of the pre-Olympics period. The city—he says—was very much like the one depicted by the director Bigas Luna in *Bilbao*, a film from 1978 starring the painter Ángel Jové and the Uruguayan actress Isabel Pisano.

"In Gerona, Roberto made friends with Ángel Jové, he always spoke to me about him and said that he had to introduce me to him because he was a very good painter," remembers Jaime. "When he got to Barcelona from Mexico, he was very young, very hopeful, and a lot of fun. He came to a friend's house and was charming, he was always a very funny guy. We had similar senses of humor so we got on well."

During the forced exile of the 1970s, in a Spain far from achieving the prosperity that would make it one of the leading countries of Europe in the '90s, solid friendships were forged quickly, within a few minutes of the parties meeting.

Jaime Rivera's voice has the tone of shared poverty, the humility of men who don't discuss their dreams of success and fame perhaps because they don't even dare to dream of them in secret.

Rivera, who was also friends with Roberto's mother, makes a face when Victoria is brought into the conversation. He thinks that Roberto loved his mother like a dutiful son, but wonders why he didn't leave her more money.

"Those are the kinds of things we don't understand about Roberto. He did some very strange things," he says remorsefully.

"There were a lot of misunderstandings with Victoria," he continues. "Maybe because Roberto had a very macho side. When his mother was in Barcelona, she met a guy who was much younger than her and they started seeing each other. Roberto couldn't take that. The apartment on Gran Vía was very large and there was a hall, I remember that you had to greet Victoria first and then talk to Roberto; they had burned their bridges."

Jaime and Roberto met up in Barcelona a few days before the writer's death. They spoke in a bar for hours. Bolaño drank his usual chamomile tea and the painter had coffee. "Victoria told me that he fell apart in a week. It didn't occur to me that he was going to die, he died suddenly."

From Rivera's point of view, Roberto Bolaño lived ironically, he was full of black humor and especially laughed at himself.

RIVERA: We spoke a lot. Very similar things had happened to us. When he was stopped in Chile, he was on a bus from the south. The soldiers made him get off and took him away and the same thing happened to me. My mother was the headmistress at a school in the south, and when I was on my way to Barcelona I went to say goodbye, and as we were coming back they picked up everyone who was young with long hair. They let me go, but he was imprisoned for a week.

The two Chileans didn't speak much about Chile. They were, he says, quite critical of their compatriots.

Roberto and Jaime found the Chileans who went to Barcelona "unpleasant people." And as Bolaño told a Chilean television program: "One of the things that I said to myself the other day when I went to Chile was that it was very strange to be surrounded by Chileans. I'm used to being the only Chilean. To me, to be Chilean is to be the only one. I was very often called 'The Chilean.' Who's the Chilean? Me. I've always lived overseas. There might have been an Argentinian around, because Argentinians get everywhere."[1]

As for Rivera's take on his countrymen and how Bolaño fit the mold: "It's worth saying that you have to be careful with how you treat Chileans, they take offense over nothing. I have a group of painters, and they're all Argentinians, it's five Argentinians and me and I have a close relationship with them. With Chileans I have to watch my words, but with the Argentinians if something annoys me I'll say so and they'll understand, they're more direct. Roberto was like that."

But, as you might expect, Bolaño didn't really fit a type, national or otherwise. He was also one of those "special" guys who always carried a notebook around with him. He wrote in it all day but didn't discuss what he had written. He was a "sponge," according to Rivera. He asked a lot of questions, and the many anecdotes told to him by such friends as Rivera were scribbled down in a notebook and later appeared in his books.

One such anecdote appears in Bolaño's novella *Distant Star*, when Carlos Wieder organizes an exhibition of photographs of people murdered in a sinister guest room in Providencia.

> RIVERA: I'd told Roberto that many years ago I had gone to an apartment in Calle Seminario and remembered a fascist painter perfectly. I continued to go to classes for a year after the coup and there was a former soldier who studied fine art with me. So, one day he invited us to an exhibition he was holding in his apartment, he had set it up in his room, and there were paintings of people who had been murdered, but he had invented them; films he saw in his head. He was a very bad painter. I was extremely shaken by the experience. I don't know when I told it to Roberto. I often see myself in his stories.

This tendency to "fictionalize" real life came to Bolaño at a very early age, according to his friend from childhood in Mexico, one of the founders of Infrarealism, Rubén Medina. It also manifested in Roberto's love for war and strategy games.

During the early period in Spain when Rivera and Bolaño were closest, Roberto was especially poor and didn't eat well. As Rivera recalls, "I went to see him at the campsite [Bolaño worked as night watchman at a campsite in Castelldefels], and he always had two thermoses of coffee. He loved fried eggs with bread and spaghetti . . . simple food." Their diet improved slightly when they got an apartment on Gran Vía: "We bought pizza or made rice with steak, a normal meal, but he wasn't very interested in food. On the Rambla on Sunday nights, we went to have pizza at a place called Rivolta. It was an old pizzeria, something of a dive but very friendly."

But even later, Roberto was miserly. At his house in Blanes, he would run out of gas for his stove, telling Rivera, "Listen, let's go out for coffee, it's cold in here." Eventually, the question of food became moot: there wasn't a movie he hadn't seen or a book he hadn't read.

"One day, I went to Blanes and drank two coffees with milk and he had two teas," River says. "He said that his liver had turned to dust and was having trouble with his gallbladder. I didn't know he'd been in hospital. Victoria told me that he was going to die."

RIVERA: He wore a checked jacket, polo shirt, and jeans, and very old leather moccasins that he never took off.

I spoke to Victoria on the telephone. She was in Gerona, very sick; she had cancer. It affected me very badly, I'm very paranoid about diseases. I didn't go to see him in the hospital. Also, there was the whole fame aspect, which I'm not interested in. Bruno told me that not that many famous people came, that he could at least be with Victoria and her daughter and go for a coffee. It didn't occur to me to go to his funeral.

I always said that to be a good painter you have to spend a lot of hours in the studio. He said the same thing about being a writer, that you had to spend a lot of hours working. I didn't meet the famous Roberto. When we were friends he called me Jaimbotas. We hugged when we saw each other. We laughed a lot.

Jaime and Roberto would often go sit on the beach. Sometimes they would talk about all kinds of things, at others they would sit in absolute silence.

With Roberto's books, Jaime's life expanded. "He was a master at developing things that I had experienced, which would have been lost if I hadn't shared them with him. We liked each other very much. Our time together was wonderful."

10

Prior Fervor

*The poetic tradition—Bolaño's best poetry is in his prose—
Parrian antilyricism—Immortality doesn't exist—The great
classic author—A passionate gambler—Roberto couldn't stand
Inti-Illimani*

José María Micó Juan (born in Barcelona, 1961) is a poet, literary scholar, and Spanish translator specializing in the classics of the Golden Century and the Italian Renaissance. He is a professor of literature at the Universitat Pompeu Fabra, and in 2006 received the national translation prize for his verse version of *Orlando Furioso* by Ludovico Ariosto (1474–1533).

His approach to literature, as a creator and an academic, is neither pompous nor pedantic. On the contrary, it is difficult to sit down for a coffee with José María and not be amazed first by his impressive literary knowledge and then the measured speech with which he seeks in vain to restrain his passion for good writers.

These include, of course, Roberto Bolaño, of whom he was first a born admirer, having enjoyed his books, and later a close acquaintance.

They met in 2000, and when they saw each other for the first time, Micó approached him, overwhelmed by the "prior fervor" (a quote from Borges) with which one approaches a classic.

In the sometimes rugged territory of Bolaño's literature, José María Micó recognizes, like many, some outcrops, several plains, and one or two unforgettable landscapes, but he is convinced that the work as a whole reveals the writer's truly great talent: "I read his texts with the certainty that there is a great writer behind them, not just a great work. I think that regardless of the differences between the works he wrote, even given the inconsistencies of some of his verse and prose works, there is a great writer behind all of them. His literature is all good, even though one might like some aspects more than others," he says.

It is true that Latin American literature before Bolaño didn't tend to offer many surprises, probably because Argentine literature is quite inward-looking and because it's no secret that the authors who are promoted around the world to non-Spanish markets tend to be chosen by Spanish publishers who, until very recently, managed the market exclusively.

"I don't know the entire map of Latin American literature," Micó says, "but as a reader of Bolaño I can say there are a series of ingredients that were latent in the best Ibero-American tradition: Rulfo, Borges, Cortázar. For whatever reason they had disappeared from literature, the literature of his home country of Chile, for example. Chilean literature before him had grown commercial to a great degree—at least the literature that reached Europe had."

In his eyes, Roberto Bolaño is an extraordinary Chilean author with elements of Mexican literature, someone who, like few others, had read the Ibero-American authors who came before him and almost all the contemporary European literature worth reading.

He was also a great reader of the classics, as is demonstrated by the list of his favorite books, drawn up at the request of *Playboy México* in 2002. He was asked to send in a list of ten, but Bolaño being Bolaño, he chose not to conform to the preestablished format. The sixteen books he chose are:

1. *Don Quixote*, Miguel de Cervantes
2. *Moby-Dick*, Herman Melville
3. The complete works of Jorge Luis Borges
4. *Hopscotch*, Julio Cortázar
5. *A Confederacy of Dunces*, John Kennedy Toole
6. *Nadja*, André Breton
7. *War Letters*, Jacques Vaché

8. *The Ubu Plays*, Alfred Jarry
9. *Life A User's Manual*, George Perec
10. *The Castle* and *The Trial*, Franz Kafka
11. *Aphorisms*, Georg Cristoph Lichtenberg
12. *Tractatus Logico-Philosophicus*, Ludwig Wittgenstein
13. *The Invention of Morel*, Adolfo Bioy Casares
14. *The Satyricon*, Petronius
15. *The History of Rome*, Livy
16. *Thoughts*, Blaise Pascal

To his friend José María, it was Bolaño's poetic soul that made him extraordinary and allowed him to create the powerful voice that changed the course of contemporary Latin American literature.

MICÓ: He was somewhat like Augusto Roa Bastos, Shakespeare's translator, and he had a lot of Jorge Luis Borges, and I'm one of those who thinks that Borges's poetry is better than his prose. The traditions of two separate genres come together in Bolaño in a much more natural way than with Borges, or Roa Bastos, and also Julio Cortázar, who produced an interesting body of poetic work.

There's a poetic foundation to Bolaño's literary work, not just in terms of the plot but also aesthetics: Bolaño's best poetry is in his prose, and his prose has that occasionally uninhibited rhythm that we attribute to poetry. There has never been another as good as Bolaño at uniting the two elements: the narrative and lyrical pulses, even though he was a lyrical poet who said several times that he was antilyrical and his favorite poet was the antipoet Nicanor Parra. In spite of all these ingredients, his literature is more than either: his novels are more than novels, and his poetry is more than poetry.

Roberto Bolaño is often compared with Julio Cortázar, and many critics believe him to be his heir. Where the Argentine and Chilean meet is in their attitude toward writing: like "nailing a cross to one's jaw," according to Roberto Arlt, whom Roberto also admired greatly.

Bolaño, who often spoke about "slapping around" writers who are tempted to discuss their own posterity, would have rather, when it came to criticism, "that they hit me in the face like Robert De Niro in *Raging Bull* and not the liver, because mine is pretty sick." He said this on the Chilean television program *Off the Record* in 1998. He has the power and strength of the great writers, he believed, his literature a whirlwind often combining with great natural disasters, the tremors of earth and heaven that one can only survive through huge effort.

He roundly refused to consider posterity. "In four million years the worst writer in Chile will have disappeared, but so will Shakespeare, so will Cervantes," he said on the television program. "We're all condemned to oblivion, not just a physical disappearance, but a total one. Immortality doesn't exist. And that's a paradox that writers know well and they suffer on account of it. There are writers who do everything they can to achieve recognition, immortality—a grandiose word if ever there was one. Meaningless, too. Immortality doesn't exist. In the long term, Shakespeare and John Doe are one and the same; nothing."

Bolaño rejected posterity so forcefully, according to Rodrigo Fresán, "because one never knows what's going on in anyone else's head, [and] because he was sure he would achieve it."

MICÓ: I say in one of my verses that an early death is the only way to achieve eternal youth, and that might be worth something to ordinary people but to writers it's different. In my classes I say that a classic is a classic only when one dies; for a writer to become a classic the first thing they need to do is die—to write first, of course, but then to die. When the death isn't a natural one, but extemporaneous in some way, as was the case with Roberto, an almost morbid phenomenon occurs in which he is "recovered" afterward, as though he were unknown before. However, what Roberto Bolaño wrote before he died was so impressive that you can't say his death had any effect: in the long term, his death, that he died at fifty, will be seen as unimportant. A little while ago, I was flicking through a novel by Jorge Ibargüengoitia, and I remembered that he had died young but I didn't remember that it had been in a legendary plane crash from when I was young, an Avianca plane [...] In the case of Ibargüengoitia, like that of Roberto Bolaño, his early death is insignificant. Of course there is work that supports it all and his early death has very quickly become an anecdote. His sadly posthumous fame is sustained not because of the circumstances of his death but his literary quality. Perhaps one day we'll get lucky and people will stop talking about how García Lorca died. It may be important in terms of understanding some aspects of Spanish history but it has nothing to do with the quality of his work.

José María Micó wasn't a close friend of Roberto Bolaño but he often met him. He attended long, intimate gatherings with friends they had in common, such as Carmen Pérez de Vega, Consuelo Gaytán, and Ignacio Echevarría.

MICÓ: On those occasions I came to realize, without knowing that he was going to die young, that in fact we were closer friends than we thought or suspected. We respected and liked each other quite a lot more than we showed because we weren't officially close friends. I also have a posthumous fondness for him because they were strange times for me. I didn't just see a lot of him but plenty of other writers and people from the literary world for the Biblioteca Breve award, and at events that the Casa de América organized. I invited him to come to the university several times. Once, he didn't even come as the main event but moderated a round table of young Colombian writers, which he did very modestly. At the time I was finishing my translation of *Orlando Furioso*, a classic of the Italian Renaissance, and he always used to ask how the translation was going, a surprising question from any other contemporary Spanish or Latin American writer, and I was always touched. I told him about where I was with it in detail, and we had conversations in which it was obvious that he not only knew who Ludovico Ariosto was but had read *Orlando Furioso*. He also knew *The Divine Comedy* very well. This showed me that he had a respect he didn't express but must have felt for me, which might also have led to a fondness that I reciprocated. I respected him for his knowledge, especially of things I knew nothing about, such as famous battles from the Second World War.

Sometimes he was passionate like a gambler, which means he got arbitrarily passionate about certain arguments. We disagreed about music. He was Chilean, and ever since I came of intellectual age, almost since I was fifteen, I have believed that one of the best musicians I know is a man called Horacio Salinas, Inti-Illimani's musical director. Roberto was a rock fan and couldn't stand Inti-Illimani. I think that we basically agreed because I was interested in the classics and he privately thought that he had the heart of a classicist—we were on the same team as Dante, Borges, Ariosto—and that his work had the potential to achieve a certain longevity. I don't know if he was convinced of it, but I was privately convinced that his work deserved to be treated as such.

11

The False Executor

The influence of Kurt Vonnegut—Rearranging the literary canon—The myth of lost youth—A surreal duel—Parrian mischief—Camilo Sesto—A new narrative syntax

In every friendship worthy of the name, only the friends involved know how deep their empathy and fondness goes. In the case of the Catalan critic Ignacio Echevarría, born in Barcelona in 1960, his role tends to be either overestimated or dismissed as a mere critic of Bolaño's work, depending on who is making the judgment.

He himself makes sure to disavow the closeness of his friendship and intimacy with the author to whom he now dedicates himself with monkish devotion, saying whenever he can that he was never officially named the Chilean writer's executor.

It is mentioned in one of the few interviews given by Carolina López, Bolaño's widow, published in the newspaper *La Vanguardia* on December 29, 2010. "Did Bolaño name a literary executor?" asks the journalist Josep Massot. She answers:

LÓPEZ: No, no. A literary executor is a legal figure and Roberto never put something in writing, and never even mentioned it. Roberto knew that I had no experience in the world of publishing, and so he said to me that if I needed help I should go to his friend Ignacio Echevarría, who published his reviews in *El País*. That's in the "Note from the Author's Heirs" in *2666*, which was published in the first edition of that novel. I asked for his help in making an inventory. Before that, on his own initiative, he put together the book *Between Parentheses* and, after the inventory, *The Secret of Evil*. His work supporting the publication of *2666* came about through Jorge Herralde. In truth, he was always closer to the publisher. The claim that Roberto named Ignacio Echevarría as his executor is a misunderstanding that I think he has tried to deny more than once. Roberto was very clear that if things went badly I, and then the children, would be responsible for his work. In the last interview he gave, he was asked: "Whose opinion of your work do you value the most?" He answered: "Carolina reads my books, and then Herralde does, and then I try to forget them forever."

Echevarría, who is often identified in articles as "Bolaño's guardian" or "curator of his work," if not directly his executor, has never sought the title that would officially tie him to his friend. He has not been able to avoid, however, being trapped in the bright white flame that burns, sometimes consistently and at others in trembling bursts, around the author's memory.

When Carolina López says that Ignacio prepared *Between Parentheses* "on his own initiative," she may be referring to the fact that the literary critic was actively assisted by Carmen Pérez de Vega, a companion who was crucial to Roberto's final years.

The issue is simply an unresolved private matter that would have nothing to do with the work if it weren't for the fact that the writer's death created a clash between two parties, each claiming to be acting according to Bolaño's wishes and intentions.

Ignacio, a friend of Carmen Pérez de Vega's, seems to have been trapped in the middle of the posthumous, senseless tangle. It is even more ironic when one considers that Bolaño wanted to leave everything settled before his death.

The controversy spread to include the Mexican writer Jorge Volpi, who did not just address an angry letter to the editor in *Letras Libres*, but also refused to acknowledge the presence of Bolaño's companion Pérez de Vega in Roberto's life.

"I always saw Bolaño with Carolina, I had no idea that he was with someone else," Volpi said in an interview.[1]

Regardless, the friendship between Bolaño and Echevarría was a powerful bond that was certainly enhanced by their literary exchanges but rooted in the characteristics they shared. These included their passion, their willingness to hold forth risky opinions, and their judgment, which in Ignacio's case was more measured but just as mordant, while Roberto's pronouncements were the fruits of his well-known, lethal spontaneity.

In a period of uncritical, whitewashed literature, Echevarría's is an original, solid, and independent voice. He is an intelligent, cultured man who writes well and analyzes his contemporaries even better, without ever condescending to his friends or worrying how his opinions might go down in circles of power—those people who commission articles, pay advances, deliver awards, and write up lists of "must read" authors.

Echevarría offers passionately expressed opinions and analysis. He has occasionally paid a high price for it, such as his painful departure in 2004 from *El País*, which also owned the publisher Alfaguara at the time. The critic described the incident as "censorship and the intentional infringement of my right to freedom of expression."

The fiery confrontation with the editors of the newspaper originated in Echevarría's unfavorable review of a book by the Basque writer Bernardo Atxaga, *El hijo del acordeonista* (The Accordion Player's Son), a review the management at *El País* described as "cruel" at best. After this review of a book by a figure considered by *El País* as untouchable, and who was also an Alfaguara author, Echevarría was frozen out from the newspaper for three months. Not suprisingly, he quit soon afterward.

Echevarría was involved in another public dispute with Jorge Volpi when the critic published his opinion of *Palabras de América* (Words of America) in the Chilean newspaper *La Nación*, on

April 18, 2004. The book was a collection of texts by the authors who took part in a gathering in Seville in 2003, in what turned out to be Bolaño's final public appearance before he died a few weeks later. The key passage of Echevarría's review:

> There they all are, cheeping next to the master: "Is it me, master? Is it me?" assuming one another to be the chosen ones, invoking the powers of their church (or parish, as applicable). And there was Roberto, laughing—How could they not have noticed?—at all of them, friends and enemies, smart and stupid alike, saying things like: "Young writers dedicate their bodies and souls to sales," "Literature, especially in Latin America, is social success," "All we're interested in is success, money and respectability," "One must sell oneself before they, whoever they are, lose interest in the purchase," or "If we could crucify Borges, we'd crucify him: we are the timid murderers, the prudent murderers."

This was the paragraph that seems to have upset Volpi.

Volpi answered in a column titled "Against Ignacio Echevarría," published in June 2004 in the Spanish edition of the Mexican magazine *Letras Libres*: "We will never know why Bolaño really went to Seville. Although it might upset Echevarría, the only thing that the writers who attended the congress had in common was a sincere admiration for him and his work. And, at least from what I could see, Roberto had an excellent time talking to all of us. That was all." This text by the Mexican sealed an enmity that remains to this day.

Echevarría may well have been a character in *The Savage Detectives*. In one chapter, a character named Iñaki Echevarne appears, whom many readers have associated with the Catalan critic. Echevarría denies that the character was inspired by him, although he has never been able to cast off the association with the famous novel. According to Ignacio, Bolaño had sketched out the famous passage on the sword fight between Iñaki Echevarne and Belano before they met personally.

The following is my interview with Echevarría.

MARISTAIN: *Would you say that you are the foremost expert on Roberto Bolaño's work?*

ECHEVARRÍA: No, not at all. I don't think that at all. There are a lot of people who know Roberto's work much better than me. Now more than ever. There are genuine experts in Bolaño's work.

MARISTAIN: *Experts or obsessives?*

ECHEVARRÍA: Both. Expertise surely garnered through obsession, but nonetheless there are people who know a lot about Roberto's work. Carmen [Pérez de Vega], Bruno [Montané], and Rodrigo [Fresán] certainly know more than I do.

MARISTAIN: *What is the best way to read Bolaño's work?*

ECHEVARRÍA: When I am asked where to start with reading Bolaño, what the best way into his world is, I say *The Savage Detectives*. The brilliance of the novel and especially its start . . . well, if that doesn't get you hooked on Bolaño's world, then nothing will. Another good way in would be the stories, but they're less easy to take in isolation from the rest of the work, and less personal. I think that the start of *The Savage Detectives* would seduce any reader; it has a lot to do with Roberto's success. For young people, that diary is a key text.

MARISTAIN: *Is that how you were seduced by Roberto's literature?*

ECHEVARRÍA: Well, no, the first one I read was *Distant Star*. I liked that book, but I must admit I wasn't that enthusiastic about it. I liked it, it was very much influenced by Borges, I read it as part of my job, to do the review, and then I read *Nazi Literature in the Americas*, which I also liked, but I still saw him as writing in Borges's shadow, he had a certain ironic detachment from literature, and the truth is that I didn't see the distinctive hallmarks of Bolaño until later. I only realized that he was an exceptional writer when I read *The Savage Detectives*.

MARISTAIN: *Borges was God to him, wasn't he?*

ECHEVARRÍA: Yes, I think that he was one of the clearest influences. There are a lot, some that are very important but are deep beneath the surface. I always discuss the influence of an author who is rarely mentioned: Kurt Vonnegut. Especially when you read Vonnegut after reading Bolaño; it's very tangible. In any case, Bolaño was a compulsive reader and he was surrounded by different voices. But one of the influences that he acknowledges, which provided a foundation for his literature, is undoubtedly Borges. When one reads *Nazi Literature in the Americas*, one can clearly see the Borges of *A Universal History of Infamy*, and the more comical Borges in the chronicles of Bustos Domecq, which he wrote with Bioy Casares. The laughter you can hear in those texts is very Bolaño-esque.

MARISTAIN: *To say that Borges was God is a way of saying that he adopted a dissident canon, which—and I don't know to what degree— he filled with his own writers, traveling companions, and colleagues whom he supported . . .*

ECHEVARRÍA: I don't think that he ever experienced the unanimous acclaim that we saw after his death. As big as his ego
might have been, and it didn't seem that big, I don't think that
he was ever aware of it ... He never even had an idea of how
central he would be, especially after *2666*. I think that Roberto,
from very early on, even before he was first published and then
before he became famous, placed himself on his own literary
map, like any great writer. And like every great writer, he rearranged and made some changes to the canon. Not so much
because he thought of himself as a canonical author, but just
to find a place for himself. I think that all conscientious writers do this to some extent. Roberto was also influenced by the
habits he acquired as an avant-garde poet in Mexico—in other
words, methods that were very derogatory to some and very
friendly to others. Part of a framework of complicity and hostility that doesn't exist today. One of the most charming things
about Roberto was that he revived a kind of maximalist attitude
regarding both his devotions and hatreds, which usually lie
somewhat dormant under the blanket of courtesy characteristic
of our culture. I think that he had a clear "with me or against
me" attitude, very much that of an avant-garde poet, which was
transferred to a great extent to his fiction, not so militantly but
with just as much attitude, because he saw himself as a public
writer. One must bear in mind that Bolaño's stance as a public
writer was built up in essentially four or five years, no more. He
was an obscure, almost secret writer until 1997 or 1998. After
that, and this is the fascinating thing about a book like *Between
Parentheses*, which includes all his appearances in the press: a
person who had been completely invisible starts to be seen, and
you can see how he develops a strategy of affinities and incli-
nations. I'm sure that he didn't have the least idea how prominent it would become.

MARISTAIN: *Did you talk about the writers he included in his canon? Did you exchange opinions on Ricardo Piglia or César Aira, for example?*

ECHEVARRÍA: Not a lot, actually. I have to admit that I have a terrible memory, so what I'm saying is somewhat hypothetical. The truth is that I didn't discuss literature with Roberto very much. We spoke about it occasionally, inevitably, but our discussions were mainly about other things. I can't remember talking about those authors, except in some cases when it was clear already that we both liked both of them very much.

MARISTAIN: *Which authors did you both like?*

ECHEVARRÍA: Rodrigo Fresán, Rodrigo Rey Rosa—the authors we had a chance to meet personally. But I don't remember talking to Roberto about Piglia, Aira, or even Enrique Vila-Matas.

MARISTAIN: *How much influence do you think that the Infrarealists really had on Bolaño's work?*

ECHEVARRÍA: Let's see, influence … I'd say that the poetic activism of Bolaño's youth helped him to create his own mythology. He built a myth about himself, about his youth. At the center of Bolaño's work is the myth of a lost youth, a brave, committed youth in which literature was linked to the overall experience. It was a myth that worked inside Roberto and fed his literature. In that sense, the role of the Infrarealists was fundamental because all the romanticism of Roberto's work is related to his own memories of a wild youth. It was a decisive influence on the construction of the central part of his narrative, which then became a kind of melancholic extension of his youth. He converts Mexico and his youth in Mexico into a personal myth and builds a good part of his literature on top of that. As a poet, I think it is very important in the same sense: he starts out as an avant-garde poet and then becomes a little less so; a poet who reflects melancholically on the avant-garde and especially everything that came with the avant-garde. And I think you could say that the influence of the movement was also down to the fact that it was derivative of the great avant-garde movements of the interwar years, which were in turn inspired by the great burst of poetry by Arthur Rimbaud and Charles Baudelaire, poets who are at the heart of Roberto's work.

MARISTAIN: *Also, Infrarealism never created its own aesthetic, did it?*

ECHEVARRÍA: No, because it was an attitude. Infrarealism was a kind of swan song for the avant-garde in Latin America, where the avant-garde, as in Spain, had a difficult existence.

MARISTAIN: *How did you meet Roberto?*

ECHEVARRÍA: I met him at the launch for *Phone Calls*. I'd been invited by Jorge Herralde because he had liked my review a lot and suggested introducing me to him. I went with Ignacio Martínez de Pisón,[2] and we met Roberto there.

MARISTAIN: *Did you get on immediately?*

ECHEVARRÍA: Yes. We went to dinner after the launch and that same night he told me he was finishing a novel in which I was a character. He told me that he would send the part that included me to see what I thought, which he did. I read the famous duel scene and told him that even without reading the rest of the novel it seemed complete nonsense, an opinion I still have. The story of the duel seems completely out of place in *The Savage Detectives*.

MARISTAIN: *Why?*

ECHEVARRÍA: Because it's completely ridiculous and a little hallucinatory in a novel in which the ridiculous and hallucinatory don't play much of a role.

MARISTAIN: *And what was Roberto's reaction?*

ECHEVARRÍA: He laughed a lot and, of course, ignored me completely. I emphasize the fact that Roberto created the character inspired by me before we had met. It was created from snippets of gossip, and thus any resemblance to reality is purely coincidental.

MARISTAIN: *What did Roberto think of your critical pieces in* El País?

ECHEVARRÍA: He laughed a lot, especially at the negative criticism. He challenged the praise. He loved the negative aspects, like all writers. I think that Roberto's sympathy for me lay with my own personal myth, in a word that was essential to him: *courage*. I think that that is the word that best defines Roberto's literature. And he always thought that to be a literary critic and to be openly critical was a brave stance to take. I have often thought that our friendship had to do with the supposition that my work required courage. He immediately sympathized with that attitude. Also, whenever a review of mine got me in trouble with a writer he was always there laughing and supporting me. He was very brave. And would have been braver still. I think that Roberto's public appearances followed a clear trend. If one reads the interviews he gave in the last two years of his life especially, one can see that they become increasingly brutal and savage, the work of someone with nothing to lose. They are increasingly Parrian in the sense that he makes Nicanor Parra's discourse his own, it is a little disconnected but he takes on everyone. I think that he was the model, but that's pure speculation. His public position as a writer put him in a difficult position because he had seen his life as being withdrawn, that of a practically anonymous writer. If he had experienced the prominence he was beginning to achieve, I think that he would have exaggerated or faked his mischievous side. Work such as "The Vagaries of the Literature of Doom," "The Myths of Cthulhu," and "Sevilla Kills Me," his last text for public consumption, are characteristic of someone taking on all and sundry.[3]

MARISTAIN: *Which contradicts those who say that he said those things because he knew that he was going to die . . .*

ECHEVARRÍA: First, he didn't know whether he was going to die or not and had learned to live with it better than those of us who don't have a fatal disease. One mustn't forget that he fairly suicid-ally delayed the decision to have a liver transplant, which would have kept him alive, in the mid-term at least. I mean that if Ro-berto had been operated on in time and the operation, which is very risky, were a success, something not at all beyond the realms of possibility, Roberto would have been fragile, which he already was, but his life would have been extended. He wasn't beset by imminent death. Death was closer to him than it is to us, but it wasn't as though he was expected to die the next day or the day after that, not even when he did die. In fact, all his friends agree upon their surprise at Roberto's death. He had never given the sense of writing for posterity, and had been working right to the end on a deliriously complex and ambitious work. It is the kind that no one sets out to write thinking that they won't be around to finish it.

MARISTAIN: *We laughed a lot when I told him that Camilo Sesto had successfully undergone a transplant ...*

ECHEVARRÍA: Carmen [Pérez de Vega] knows much more about this than I do, but I think that his reluctance to be operated on was due to the fact that liver operations have a certain margin of error, a significant margin when it is a matter of life or death or very serious. So, deciding what day you roll the dice to determine whether you'll become an invalid or die, even though you know it could be your salvation, is a decision that one puts off. And he delayed the decision suicidally. An early death beatifies artists. There are plenty of examples. You can still find people who say that all the fuss over Roberto's work is occurring in great measure because of his early death, his wild youth ... that if Bolaño had lived to eighty, he would, like all writers, have witnessed his eclipse or the waning of his star. And it's a legitimate point of view. One pays for their beauty with their death, which is a very high price. But Roberto would write with one foot in the grave, and I think that that's something he can't be reproached or criticized for. It was his condition. Others write with the desperation of hunger or to achieve fame. He wrote with the desperation to finish his work. It wasn't a marked card; it was the card he was dealt.

MARISTAIN: *What did you like about Roberto?*

ECHEVARRÍA: A lot of things. It's very difficult to talk about now, but I felt a great affection for him. He was a very fun person with whom you could laugh a lot. You could be sure to laugh with

Roberto. I have to mention my regret that my relationship with Roberto was quite short. He was very charming but I didn't see him that often, as he lived in Blanes. In the final years, because he had to go to Barcelona to see the doctor quite often, I saw more of him. But going up to Blanes specifically to see Roberto was something I did four or five times a year at the most. In retrospect, that weighs down on me, because it was a very fun thing to do. As I never had the feeling that Roberto was going to die, I didn't guard our friendship jealously. Roberto loved to talk on the phone, which I hate. Sometimes I'd be working at my desk and get a call from Roberto, which meant at least an hour's conversation, so I didn't pick up. So I missed out on the chance to talk to him much more than I did. I don't feel anything about that. I had the relationship with him that I was supposed to have. I don't feel that I should have been with him more because he was going to be great or famous. I also have to say, and I've said so many times, that I have absorbed Roberto's greatness over time, posthumously. *The Savage Detectives* is a novel that, when you reread it, as I did a short while ago, you find has grown. It hasn't stopped growing since it was published. When I reviewed it, calling it a stupendous work, I had no idea, or very little idea, of how important it would be, what a crucial role it was going to play, or the greatness of the writer that lay behind it. While I was his friend, I didn't have the sensation when I was with him that I was in the presence of a great writer. I saw him as a good writer, of course, but I didn't get the thrill that I would get now if we could meet. Neither am I one for idolatry. I try not to be avaricious about these things. I never thought that I should spend more time with him so as to have more anecdotes. That never occurred to me. I don't regret that.

MARISTAIN: *How did you react when you read 2666?*

ECHEVARRÍA: I was stunned. I reread *The Savage Detectives* last year and that stunned me too. I remembered that novel very well but, I'm telling you, it was as though it had grown. But it really hit me that I didn't know who I had been talking to when I read *2666*. In retrospect, you can see the power of that book in the ones that came before it. Everything is read in the light of that one. That's when I realized, somewhat late, which doesn't say much for my perspicacity, that an extraordinary author had died.

MARISTAIN: *And then one terrible day Roberto died and you were presented to the press as the executor of his work . . .*

ECHEVARRÍA: Yes, but I bear no responsibility for that. In fact, I found out from Carolina López herself that he had recommended me for help in publishing issues. That had nothing to do with my being named his executor, which is a legal personage that must be notarized and formalized. So Carolina consulted me on Roberto's recommendation for as long as she saw fit. When she decided that I couldn't help her anymore, she stopped asking. The press getting the idea that I was Bolaño's executor was more down to Carolina than me, because I have always been very aware of the power of that word and I never felt like Roberto's executor. I think that when a lot of people refer to me as the executor, they use the word as if it meant a person whom someone trusts. Immediately after Roberto's death, what I felt was an urge to gather his disparate work in the press. I proposed publishing *Between Parentheses* to Carolina and she was skeptical but let me do it, and today I think that it was a good idea. I think that when people started to discuss where Roberto and his work stood, *Between Parentheses* helped to draw the map a little. It's a slightly discredited map. I've talked about this with Rodrigo [Fresán] quite often, because many of the texts were one-offs and there are different tones and contexts in the book. That doesn't matter. The work drew a small map with which Roberto was going to be read from then on, which would help to establish connections. What must be borne in mind is that it would lead to the recanonization of Latin American literature.

MARISTAIN: *What did you feel when you found out about the trust that your friend had placed in you, and how did it feel to lose the trust of his widow?*

ECHEVARRÍA: Well, when Carolina told me I was very flattered, although one mustn't read too much into it. I think that Roberto would have said that to her, not just on account of any trust he might have placed in me but also because he knew that I worked in the world of publishing, that I knew the ins and outs of that universe, that I got on well with his publisher Jorge Herralde, that I had experience editing texts … I suppose that all singled me out over other friends whose tastes and literary criteria may have coincided just as much or even more so with his than my own. It was a technical decision to some degree and shouldn't be seen as anything more than it is. I agreed to do it with great pleasure, but I'm not arrogant about it. When we started to publish *Between Parentheses* first, then *2666* and *The Secret of Evil*, I remember that Carolina—together with a lot of other people—thought that no one was going to be interested. They couldn't see why it was worth the trouble. There was a certain degree of skepticism about whether, now that Roberto was dead, the material, which in some cases was already well known, would be of interest, and whether it was worth publishing. They weren't expecting, and neither was I, the thirst for material like that. I didn't play the role of editor of Roberto's legacy for very long. When Carolina withdrew her confidence, I accepted it, not happily, but with a certain amount

of relief, because by now the Roberto phenomenon had started
to snowball and grow, and spending the whole day answering
questions and making decisions about Bolaño, acting as a kind of
widower to him, wasn't particularly appealing.

MARISTAIN: *But it caused something of a schism. There was a confrontation between you and Carolina. If she's there, you're not, and
vice versa . . .*

ECHEVARRÍA: Well, you'd have to ask her about that. In any case,
it's a completely unilateral decision. Carolina withdrew her confidence in me for what I think were private reasons, she'd have to
reveal them herself, and that's fine. I've been quite understanding
of the burden for Carolina to have to administer all these things
she wasn't expecting . . . I can understand that. Administering the
legacy of a writer like Roberto is a heavy burden.

MARISTAIN: *How does a critic of your standing and prestige assess the
posthumous Bolaño?*

ECHEVARRÍA: Well, I think that everything that has been published after *2666* is just an accessory. That book, in the sequence
that he published it during his life, puts the finishing touches
to the cathedral that Bolaño built. It's completed. We can add
chapels, altars, and flourishes, but nothing by Roberto that has
or will be published now will, I think, reconfigure his work. At
best it might improve understanding, add some subtleties, but the
work is there. If nothing else by Roberto were published, nothing would be lost. Now there are poems, narrative fragments, old
or forgotten novels to be published, especially diaries and correspondence. I'd be the first to read the material avidly, enjoy it,
and edit it according to what one picks up during their reading.

However, I don't think that anyone can pretend that the books published after *2666* are going to change anything. The die is cast. Bolaño's standing and place in literature have been assured by what has already been published.

MARISTAIN: *I don't know where he found the time, but Bolaño's correspondence is prolific ...*

ECHEVARRÍA: Yes. It promises to be sensational. It would be difficult to get it together and publish it in an organized fashion, even without taking into account personal issues ... Time will set everything in its place. There's no rush because, I repeat, Roberto's place is assured and the material might be useful for a biography, for future criticism, but it wouldn't matter if we had to wait to read those letters in fifteen or thirty years.

MARISTAIN: *What is the book that you're writing about Roberto going to focus on?*

ECHEVARRÍA: At the moment it's not anything. It's a friendly agreement I made with a publisher, because I have great difficulty saying no. It's something that I have in mind but I don't know what I'm going to do about it. Of course it won't be a biography because I'm not a biographer. I don't have the time or the aptitude, and I also don't think it's possible to write a biography of Bolaño right now, with all the insurmountable barriers there are. It would have to be a biography that had access to all his correspondence, all his diaries, all the testimony he left behind, as a book without that access could only be provisional. So if by some divine or Bolaño-esque inspiration I can find a niche in which to do something personal and different, I will, and it will be saved from the overflowing chest of good intentions.

MARISTAIN: *When you give talks, what do you feel? Do you enjoy talking about Bolaño?*

ECHEVARRÍA: Listen, I love talking about Bolaño, although I sometimes feel a little like I'm going on and on. I can't help it, it's not very dignified, but when you get over that, I feel very grateful to be able to talk about Bolaño because, in contrast to other subjects, the experience is almost always widely shared. He is an author people have read and it's easy to share something of him with others. It's getting increasingly difficult to say something original or new about Roberto. But fine, I am pretty long-winded and there are plenty of things that it doesn't hurt to repeat, because the legend that surrounds Roberto continuously brings up the same mistakes, the same well-intentioned lies, the same misunderstandings, and so it's not such a bad thing that some of us are taking the trouble to correct and rectify all that.

MARISTAIN: *What do you think about the canon proposed by Ro-oberto Bolaño?*

ECHEVARRÍA: Well, the important thing about Roberto since he published *The Savage Detectives* is that, for the first time since the boom, a new paradigm for writing was established on which a new map could be based. The real importance of Roberto is that both his literature and his public persona have made room for something that had to some extent been lying dormant but that no one had yet accessed. Even though between the boom and Roberto there were very great writers with very personal styles— Pedro Lemebel in Chile, César Aira and Rodolfo Fogwill in Argentina, guys who have worked very articulately and with a lot of talent on creating their public personae—in many ways it was still the big stars from the boom that people think of when they think of the Latin American writer. Suddenly Roberto Bolaño, with his romanticism, his myth of the wandering writer and associated exile, his rootlessness, his entirely eclectic literature from Europe, Latin America, Spain, and North America, discovered a new language, a new narrative syntax. Suddenly this stuck, not necessarily because he was better than any other writer. After Roberto Bolaño, the public figure of the writer exemplified by Gabriel García Márquez or Jorge Luis Borges was made to seem obsolete, antiquated.

12

When Bolaño Murdered a Skinhead

In the end, everything gets Bolaño-ized—If you don't go through Blanes you'll never get home—I've had better paellas—To the nursery for mutant writers—Never kill a child in your book—Roberto had been dead for ten years—There are worse fates—My body is screwed

Bolaño often praised the Argentine writer Rodrigo Fresán, his great friend. And the appreciation was mutual: "To my generation, Bolaño was and always will be the more talented, crazier, and essentially more honest elder brother. Bolaño wrote without limitations, without a safety net, and without stopping. Bolaño wrote as easily as he breathed, and the shock wave from the big bang that was his work will continue to expand, bouncing around all over the place for many, many years," read Fresán in his eulogy at Roberto's funeral in July 2003.

Rodrigo Fresán was just twenty-seven when he published *Historia argentina* (Argentinian Story), a book that stayed on the bestseller list for six months and was hailed as a literary revelation in 1991. These were fertile years for fiction in Argentina, produced by a generation that was born in the 1960s (a decade that saw the appearance of *Bomarzo* by Manuel Mujica Láinez, and *On Heroes and Tombs* by Ernesto Sábato, among others), which included, in addition to Fresán, Juan Forn, Alan Pauls, and Martín Caparrós, just to name a few. This was a new, powerful crop that may not have built a single aesthetic—because the authors weren't interested in that—but did manage to define a literary territory that never loses its shape or content. At the end of the day, as Rodrigo says, Argentina "is a land that gives birth to good footballers and good writers."

Yet Fresán skillfully avoids generational labels or any suggestion that he is trying to construct an ideology. As the representative of a new generation of Argentine writers, Fresán debunked myths and titles. "The idea of the new Argentine literature also has to do with the publishing and media agendas that suddenly appear at a particular moment and then leave you frozen there forever. Every morning I get up praying for a new generation of Argentine writers to appear so that I can escape the classification and get on with writing," he says. In a Borgesian kind of way, however—with the tendency to regard "Argentineness" objectively from a perspective where its national icons such as dulce de leche or soccer are challenged or ignored at will—the author of *Los jardines de Kensington* (Kensington Gardens) will always be linked to his homeland.

Having lived in Barcelona for a decade, the writer—once described as "a pop Borges" by Javier Aparicio in *El País*—has observed how his first and most celebrated book reached a maturity that makes it relevant to readers both young and old. With the mild skepticism that is his most distinctive characteristic, he can enjoy the continued interest in his groundbreaking work, which had rocketed him in the prime of his youth to the big league of a contemporary literature always on the lookout for new gods and paradigms.

About Fresán, whom Enrique Vila-Matas describes as "the author who has read Bolaño the most," Ray Lóriga wrote: "One shouldn't wait for writers to die to send them flowers, the good mental health of that Argentine is a daily gift. If he enjoys the miracle of being loved, why not love him? Praise comes easily when one is faced with talent."

In his introduction to *Historia argentina*, Ignacio Echevarría, with his customary wisdom, notes the appearance of a "new model for international writers. Writers who are disdainful of the literary establishment, invested in their own youth, making themselves into a cause and with a tendency to confuse a lack of inhibitions with rebellion."

Mass-market journalism, pop culture, rock culture (Fresán is friends with the Argentine rock stars Andrés Calamaro—about whom he has written on numerous occasions—and Fito Paéz), eclectic erudition, and auteur and commercial cinema all go into the cocktail that has made Fresán, almost in spite of himself, into a professional writer whose next novel is always eagerly awaited— at least from the outside.

Inside, there is Rodrigo the incredible reader—"No one can read as much as he can"—the man who says that he never wants to die so as not to miss out on the books still to be written, who is fond of asking people, rather than what soccer team they support, whom they prefer: Batman or Superman.

Fresán makes an appearance in the first chapter of *2666* ("The Part About the Critics"), standing with his partner looking at the statue of Peter Pan in Kensington Gardens. Bolaño also dedicated one of his regular columns in the Blanes newspaper to Rodrigo: "Everything Is in Fresán," which was published in *Between Parentheses*. In the article, Roberto says: "I laugh a lot when I speak to Fresán. We rarely mention death."

This interview with the Argentinian writer took place in Ignacio Echevarría's house in Balmes, Barcelona. It was a genuine achievement to get Rodrigo to give an interview about his dead friend. Like Juan Villoro, he is convinced that to continue talking about Bolaño in the press will just feed the legend that surrounds him.

MARISTAIN: *Did I detect a certain amount of Buenos Aires humor in your reaction to the naming of Calle Roberto Bolaño in Gerona?*

FRESÁN: No, I was thinking that when they build houses there, the most desirable address will be Roberto Bolaño 2666. I think that people will fight one another to live there. The street thing was great, it was fun, very Bolaño-esque. I think that one of Roberto's traits, which remains after his death, is that, in the end,

everything gets Bolaño-ized. When I met him, it was under very
Bolaño-esque circumstances, the kind of thing that happens all
the time with him. I think that that's part of the legacy of great
writers. Writers don't just create an important body of work, they
also manage to irradiate or pollute or change the world immediately around them a little.

MARISTAIN: *How did you meet Roberto?*

FRESÁN: I got to Barcelona in 1999 soon after I was married. I
knew Enrique Vila-Matas, the people at the publisher Tusquets,
and Jorge Herralde, who had published *Historia argentina*, so
I had a list of telephone numbers of people to call to say "I'm
here" and tell them that I'd come as a foreign correspondent for
the newspaper *Página/12*. And when I called Jorge, he said that
that afternoon he was launching a new book by Jaime Bayly. He
invited me to come and said that he'd introduce me to Roberto
Bolaño. I had read books by Bolaño: *Distant Star, Nazi Literature
in the Americas*, and *Phone Calls*. I had also just read *The Savage
Detectives*, which I had got at the Guadalajara Book Fair. There
were a few copies of it there after it won the Herralde Prize. My
favorite, not the best one, was *Distant Star*, and it still is, although
perhaps because it has that aura of emergence, because it was the
first book I read by Roberto. Often, the first book by a writer that
you enjoyed a lot occupies a special place in one's heart. So I went
to the launch for the autobiographical novel by Jaime Bayly about
his mother, and Roberto immediately invited me to have lunch
at his house the next Saturday … It was a Tuesday or Wednes-
day and he invited me very insistently, he was almost worryingly
insistent, saying that I had to come … "To Blanes?" I asked, and
he replied, "Yes, to Blanes." I told him that I would love to but
I'd only just arrived. We were staying in a temporary apartment,

and the idea of taking a train … we hadn't unpacked our bags …
We had come to live in Barcelona, and we had to do the paperwork for our residence visa. But he said that I had to come to his
house on Saturday. I worried about the train, but he said it was
very easy and then started to give me a series of extremely complicated instructions. They were contradictory instructions whose
sole purpose was to get me lost, stations where you had to change,
and when I finally got to Blanes I found that there was a much easier way to get there from Barcelona. Also, to tempt me, he said that
he was going to make a paella; the best one I'd ever had in my life,
I couldn't miss it. So Ana, my new wife, and I went to Plaza Catalunya. Following Roberto's instructions, I got off in Tarragona, in
the other direction. I called him from the station and said: "Look,
Roberto, this isn't working." It was two thirty in the afternoon, and
I said that maybe we should leave it for another day, but he answered: "It's very important that you come, you have to." I said
that I was sorry about the paella, but he said, "It is essential that
you come to visit me today, it's much more important than you
think …" So I started to get a little worried, but then he said: "If
you don't go through Blanes you'll never get home, you'll fall into
a hole in the space-time continuum and spend the rest of eternity
going round and round on the train like in *The Invention of Morel*.
"Screw it," I thought, "this guy's either a psychopath or a serial
killer." But he still managed to persuade me. So I eventually got to
his house and ate his paella, which, I have to say, was one of the
worst I've ever had in my life. I remember Carolina being so
ashamed of the paella that Roberto had made and him right in
my face saying: "Tell me that that's not the best paella you've
ever had in your life!" I told him that actually I'd had better
paellas. [*Laughs.*] But after that we started to see each other
very often. I was extremely happy after my visit. We went to
his studio across the road, and he gave me some books I didn't

have that were impossible to get at the time: *The Skating Rink*, *La senda de los elefantes* (The Elephant's Path), which was later republished as *Monsieur Pain*.

MARISTAIN: *Did you talk about literature that day?*

FRESÁN: I've often thought about why Roberto was interested in me. In fact, I don't talk about Roberto anymore—this interview is an exception—because it's got excessive and I feel bad, as if I were on some kind of stand-up comedy tour telling the same joke over and over again. But I thought that I should come here, first because of the interview you did with him, his last one, in which I saw that he was unusually interested and committed to answering you, and he says that I'm one of his best friends, among other things. It seemed as though I'd be offending his ghost if I refused on this occasion.

Getting back to the subject: why Roberto was interested in me. I think that first, he was a consummate romantic, like Nicola di Bari ... There's a very funny anecdote that I haven't told before but that explains a lot. I lived in a place very close to La Central, which was his favorite bookshop. He would order books and go to pick them up when he came to Barcelona to visit the doctor or to go to his publisher Anagrama, his two regular destinations. He would pass by my house before or afterward, sometimes calling beforehand, sometimes surprising us. We went to the bookshop together, I chose books for me, took them to the till, and he'd insist on paying. That happened the first, second, and third times, and a writer is never going to stop someone buying them books. It's a very nice thing to do, especially if it's another writer doing the buying, but one day I said to him: "Listen, Roberto, I'm very grateful, but why are you buying me books?" He replied: "Well, you're a young writer from Latin America ..." I told him that he'd made a mistake, that I'd come as a foreign correspondent for a newspaper. Also, at the time the Argentine peso was equal to the dollar so I was doing pretty well. "What's your salary?" he asked, and when I told him the figure he went bright red and spat out: "You're a shitty bourgeois aristocrat and I'm paying for your books, thinking that you were a writer fleeing from your country!" "Look," I said, "Roberto, that's you—don't confuse things." What I'm trying to say is that he, as Ignacio [Echevarría] points out quite rightly, based all his work on his youthful experiences. I think that that was also transferred to other areas too.

The second thing was that he was very interested in all things Argentinian and especially the country's literature. If an author were Argentinian he would immediately be more interested in them than any other writer in Spanish. I think that he, in Chile, and Enrique Vila-Matas here, are much closer to literature in Argentina, the great nursery of mutant writers of Latin America. What in other countries on the continent is exceptional—you'll always find two or three strange writers—in Argentina is basically normal, all the writers are like that. Normal writers in Argentina are rare in their normality. I mean I only knew Roberto between 1999 and 2003, so I was very honored by what he said in that interview ...[1] The level of intensity of a friendship is difficult to measure, but I do think that I might have been one of Roberto's last friends, which was a privilege and an honor. In the sense that I was one of the last people he opened the door to out of friendship at a time when he was a kind of Buzz Lightyear from *Toy Story*, someone who was committed to his work and who didn't need many people around him. He was pretty well served by the contacts he already had. He was essentially chained to his computer and so it gives me great pride that he decided to make space for me to discuss things that weren't necessarily literary.

MARISTAIN: *He seemed to know everything, to be up-to-date with everything...*

FRESÁN: I think that that's a quality of insomniacs. I have had three encyclopedic friends who, strangely, are all dead and all stayed up at night. At night, at the computer, with Google and nighttime channels, you take more in, and that's where the idea of the brainiac who knows everything came from. At night, also, you get bored, everyone has gone and you're alone, awake and wondering what to do. His literature, like that of Thomas Pynchon, fed on curious information and international strangeness. Keeping well informed was a part of his work. It didn't stop him from calling you at one in the morning, as if that were the most normal things in the world. Roberto died before my son was born, but I still think that it would have been pretty terrible if I had had a newborn baby and Roberto still called me in the middle of the night.

We didn't talk about literature much, I never read an unpublished text of his and he didn't read anything of mine. The only thing he read was when he came to the house unannounced and I was working on the computer, I think on *Kensington Gardens*. The computer was on and he sat down to look, without saying anything. That same day, Alan Pauls called from Buenos Aires and they met over the phone. Curiously, the person he talked to the most about his books and what he was doing was Ana, my wife, who's Mexican, and so he called her a lot to ask her things about Mexico. I remember a very long conversation between Ana and Roberto about turkey buzzards, the different kinds of turkey buzzard. They also talked about cookery recipes, ingredients and things like that. The only thing that Roberto ever wanted to know about an unpublished book was whether a child died in it or not. He used to say that a writer should never kill a child in their book. I said to him that in fact in *Kensington Gardens* a child did indeed die, and he said that in that case he would never read it. He also said that when I had a child, I'd never want to kill one in my fiction again. It's true. In fact, in the book I'm writing now I had to bend things quite considerably to keep a child alive, because you don't mess around with things like that.

MARISTAIN: *Did you ever see the famous illustrated map of Sonora he had in his study?*

FRESÁN: No. I went to his studio many times, it was a kind of cavern made of books, and I saw the blackboard with the map of *2666*. With names and arrows ...

MARISTAIN: *It's said that he wrote* 2666 *according to the rules of the war games he liked so much* ...

FRESÁN: I don't know how he wrote it. We all knew that he was working on it, he had occasional breaks to publish the books he published while he was writing that book. The only thing that he said to me about it was that I was in a part of *2666*, in "Kensington Garden," and that was it. He wasn't very interested in discussing his books. I think that he saw the writing process as something very intimate and private. Once the book was published, then we could talk about it. Once it was published he might even ask what you liked and what you didn't.

MARISTAIN: *I guess that Bolaño died thinking that the paella he made for you really was the best you'd ever had in your life* ...

FRESÁN: Yes, probably.

MARISTAIN: *He was very stubborn like that . . .*

FRESÁN: I don't know if *stubborn* is the right word. He was vehement in his opinions and he had his explosions. A conversation could be going along very placidly and suddenly he'd bang his fist on the table and set out on the warpath. The other day, watching the first part of the documentary [*Roberto Bolaño, la batalla futura*, by Ricardo House], and all the interviews with his friends, I thought about what he must have been like when he was young and healthy. The Roberto we knew was a little limited in his movements. He had an idea for an anthology of Latin American writers who were going to be organized like an army. He said that they would all be there but divided into sections: the marines, tactical troops, black ops . . . He used to say that the area he had planned out best was the Red Cross, where he was going to send all the authors he wasn't interested in. They would perform essential medical services, but he didn't want them fighting by his side.

MARISTAIN: *What happened the day he came to ring your doorbell?*

FRESÁN: That day we met in Plaza Catalunya and we went to eat at a Kentucky Fried Chicken outlet. Roberto had never eaten at a place like that so I took him for an "anthro-archaeological" experience. He couldn't believe it, it was full of Latin Americans. He said to me: "Rodrigo, this is where we always have to meet." It was pouring with rain, I left him at the station so he could go back to Blanes and I went home. Half an hour later, my doorbell rang and I went out to find Roberto looking pale and soaking wet. He asked for a cup of tea and I asked him what had happened: "I've just killed someone," he said. I froze. He had picked up some money from *Letras Libres* for a conversation we had had about

Philip K. Dick ["Two Men in the Castle: An Electronic Conver-sation about Philip K. Dick," published in the June 2002 edition of *Letras Libres*, Spain]. Roberto told me that someone had tried to steal the money, that it wasn't much but it was very important to him that the money from work we had done together didn't fall into the hands of skinheads. "They took out a knife, but I took it and stabbed one of them and he died right there in front of me." I asked him if there had been any witnesses. He said no, the plat-form was empty. So I said that certainly the security cameras at the station would have recorded something. "I don't know, I don't want to talk about that, I'm thinking of my son, of my wife, what do I do now?" I offered to go with him to the police station, tell-ing him he should turn himself in and say that it was self-defense. "An Argentinian writer turning in a Chilean writer, great. Is that all you have to say?" I said that the only other option was not to say anything and see what happens. "Fine," he said, "I won't say anything, but how can I go back home and hug my son and look him in the eye without telling him that his father is a murderer?" "Roberto," I said, "I don't know what to tell you, if I tell you to re-port it you say that I'm a traitor to the cosmic southern belt, and if I say the opposite you start talking about your son, I don't know what to do … this is very serious."

Then he sat down and asked: "How could you believe that?" I replied that it wasn't that I believed him but that I didn't un-derstand why else he would have got off the train, got himself soaking wet, and rung my doorbell with that story. He said that the train had had technical problems so he'd have to take a taxi back to Blanes, and he came here to call one but that had seemed a little vulgar so he thought he'd make it more fun. I told him to go to hell.

MARISTAIN: *He liked playing terrifying jokes like that …*

FRESÁN: Yes. I said that everything around us became a little "Bolaño-ized," and he was sort of aware of it. He liked to play those pranks sometimes. In the text that Ignacio found in *Between Parentheses* ["Everything Is in Fresán"], he ends up saying: "Strangely, Rodrigo and I never discuss death." I mean, sometimes the subject of death came up, of course, but he brought it up playfully.

MARISTAIN: *What did you learn from him, and what did you learn about him?*

FRESÁN: As a writer, what I ask from other writers is the pleasure of reading. I don't approach great writers expecting them to teach me something. What I learned from Bolaño, and I think that he is an excellent example, was seeing someone who very firmly, emphatically, and vigorously took pleasure in his work, in reading and writing. You can say that new generations were attracted to Roberto because he died young, by the idea of someone who has nothing triumphing in the end, which is very attractive to anyone who wants to be a writer, but I think that what will remain in time, once the mystique that surrounds Roberto has faded, is that when you read him, you get the urge to read and write yourself. I think that that's the best thing anyone can say about a writer.

MARISTAIN: *That was something that Bioy Casares also used to say about great writers.*

FRESÁN: Yes, I think that that's what classics are. And also that if they're really good, they achieve an even higher, rarer level where they can be read over and over again. You'll always find something new. What Calvino said is true: "A true classic is a book you never finish reading." That's quite true of Roberto. I'm also glad that I met him after I'd read four or five books by him. That allowed me to avoid succumbing to our friendship and intimacy, and to see and judge him objectively.

MARISTAIN: *Are you a different writer after knowing him?*

FRESÁN: No. I think that if a friend were to tell him that he had changed the way he wrote after meeting him, he'd raise his eyebrows and slap them around.

MARISTAIN: *I mean that maybe the voracious way he wrote, spending ten hours a day in front of the computer, might make someone who, I don't know, writes four hours a day, for example . . .*

FRESÁN: I don't know whether he expected to die soon, and also I don't know whether all that grotesque, clownish talk about his imminent death with his friends was a form of exorcism. As though if he talked about it a lot it wouldn't happen. Writers have those tics, a little savant, a little dumb . . . but there was something about him that felt that he was writing against something, as fast as possible. I don't know if he thought faster than he could physically write and was thus always competing with himself, against the ideas of a gigantic brain, I don't know. Ten years before Roberto died, he had his first hepatic attack that almost killed him, and he was certain that if he went back into the hospital he would die, which was true in the end. I said to him, "Roberto, stop screwing around, sign the forms, just to see what happens, they make medical advances every day," but he refused. Also, Roberto liked Philip K. Dick a lot and had a very philipkdickian suspicion that he had died during the first liver attack, and that everything that had happened to him in the subsequent ten years was the life that he hadn't been able to experience in reality. I said to him that it was a little unpleasant of him to say things like that, because they meant that I was just a character of his, that we're all just his fantasies. He replied: "Well, Rodrigo, it's better than being one of Isabel Allende's characters. There are worse fates …"

MARISTAIN: *He was right …*

FRESÁN: I don't know, I don't go around saying "that's good" or "that's bad." The supposedly unwritten ending of *2666* apparently had something to do with posterity and an Arturo Belano converted into a kind of superbeing, transmitting the entirety of *2666* à la Kubrick, like a kind of floating fetus in a space station. One thing I do remember happened in a bar on the corner of the street where he lived. It was one of the last times we spoke, there was another friend there who became his friend too, Alfredo Garófano, who's a paparazzo. He started to think about the future and fantasized about the idea of living in a time when he could transcend his own body and be attached to a metallic structure … "My body is screwed," he said. And he also said how happy he would be inside a Terminator-style shell, writing from within a casing that made him immortal.

MARISTAIN: *His celebrated cinematic knowledge, was that true or was it more like his best paella in the world?*

FRESÁN: No, he knew a lot about cinema. He watched a lot of films at night, rented a lot of videos and loved bad films. I remember a conversation on a train with Ignacio when we were on our way to Mataró to launch a book of mine and Roberto came with us for some of the trip. During the four stations we shared, he decided to describe a film version of Dante's *Divine Comedy*

in detail. He told us about scenes, camera angles, et cetera. I said
to him: "Roberto, that film doesn't exist." His reply was "Rodrigo,
I've seen it." He spoke about the director, the actors. Of course,
when I got home I looked for it and it did indeed exist.[2] Also, you
couldn't get copies of the film anymore and it was only shown
on television. That was more unsettling than if he had made the
whole thing up.

MARISTAIN: *How about music, seeing as how you're an expert on the
subject?*

FRESÁN: Well, he had horrible taste in music. Obviously he liked
Johnny Cash and Bob Dylan but also some Mexican rock that
he didn't just sing to me but also mimicked the actions, doing
the screams. He terrified me when he did that, he was scary. He
looked like a psychopath who'd take out a knife and gut you there
and then. The songs had horrible lyrics; a very pedestrian kind
of punk, very vulgar, awful. He liked Elvis a lot. The last band he
became a fan of was Morphine. I loaned him the records and he
never returned them. The singer from Morphine [Mark Sand-
man] died in Italy in 1999 and I think that attracted him too.
That was something that happened with Roberto: you'd visit him
one day and find him pale. He'd say that he was dying and you'd
laugh. So one day, in the backseat of Garófano's car, he was lying
back listening to a record by Bob Dylan that had just come out,
it must have been *"Love and Theft"* from 2001. So he was lying in
the back, as though on his deathbed, and improvising grandiose
statements. I told him to stop screwing around and he said things
like: "A golden light, a golden light covers me and surrounds
me in the moment ... Bob, Bob, Dylan, Dylan, I deliver myself
to you ..." Suddenly there was an ominous silence, it was night,
and we started to say his name but he didn't answer. Alfredo and

I looked at each other, until he finally woke up and said, "Scary, isn't it?" He was always playing those kinds of pranks.

MARISTAIN: *So sometimes you wanted to throttle the child inside him . . .*

FRESÁN: [*Laughs.*] He was obsessed with the Argentine critic Graciela Speranza, whom he'd never met in his life. He'd call me at midnight and speak in a very poor Argentine accent: "Rodrigo, it's Graciela Speranza, I'm in Barcelona." I know Graciela Speranza, she has a very deep voice, and so I told Roberto that that wasn't her voice. "Rodrigo," he says, "what are you saying, why don't you answer me? I'm going to go back to Buenos Aires and I'm going to tell everyone how awful you are." He did things like that. He loved *Big Brother* and reality shows in general, he saw them as the freaks from *The Martian Chronicles*, I think, as characters.

MARISTAIN: *If he had any idea of his success, he didn't mention it, did he?*

FRESÁN: If you're asking me whether he acted like a successful person, the answer is no. One thing that I admired very much about him was that he never acted like a Latin American writer, with all his overseas followers, he never made use of that character, which I think could have helped him.

MARISTAIN: *And was he as austere in his habits as he said?*

FRESÁN: Well, I think that Roberto was very much marked by his experience of poverty. If you were ever very poor in your life, your needs become minimal.

MARISTAIN: *Do you miss him?*

FRESÁN: Very much. I miss him in every way. I also miss the books he might have written. The loss of Roberto is that of a writer with two hundred books ahead of him. He scaled a peak, but he might have climbed more. I read *Woes of the True Policeman*, which I think is a horrible title, but the book is great. I would have liked Roberto to meet my son, to see him, play with him; he was a lot of fun with children. Of course I miss him as a friend. My wife's whole family is in Mexico and mine is in Argentina, so when the phone rings at a certain hour you think that something has happened to someone in the family. In my case, for a long time every time the phone rang at night or early in the morning, I thought that it was Roberto.

13

"These days it's very easy to say that you were a friend of Bolaño's"

The great Mexican author—The inevitable Cortázar—A critical sanctification—Brilliant and erudite—Sentimental attraction—Like a pop star—The postpolitical writer—Continuity with magical realism—The power of money—The anthology of Latin American writers—Seville kills me—The last Latin American writer

"I started to read Bolaño quite early on. I was living in Spain at the time, doing a doctorate in Salamanca and writing *En busca de Klingsor* [In Search of Klingsor]. When *Nazi Literature in the Americas* came out, I read it without knowing anything about it, just because the title seemed to be related to the book I was writing. I immediately thought that he was a fantastic author."

These are the words of the writer Jorge Volpi (born in Mexico, 1968), a determined advocate of Roberto Bolaño's literature. He was a producer of the documentary *Roberto Bolaño, la batalla futura*, when he ran a cultural TV channel in Mexico, the 22.

Volpi believes that *Distant Star* is one of Bolaño's best works and *2666* his best: "It was a revelation to read it after Roberto's death, and I think that in spite of its success it hasn't yet been read properly. It opens many different doors for literature, not just Latin American literature."

After that first read of *Nazi Literature in the Americas*, Volpi couldn't stop reading Bolaño. They also built up a personal relationship—which never dimmed the Mexican's fascination with the Chilean's literature—as they kept meeting in different places.

"These days it's very easy to say that you were a friend of Bolaño's, but we at least had a continuous personal relationship for several years, until very shortly before his death. He always surprised, fascinated, and moved me to the end," he says.

Volpi thinks that the entire imaginative universe in Bolaño's literature was located in Mexico. He often noted his reluctance to return to the country that gave him so much material for his books.

"He was invited to Guadalajara [the book fair] several times and always canceled," he says. "I think that was because his imaginative world was still Mexico. Of course, he wrote Chilean and Argentinian books with characters from throughout Latin America, even Catalan books, but the center of his imaginative world, as seen in *The Savage Detectives* and *2666*, was still Mexico, and that, of course, makes him a great Mexican writer."

In the essay "El insomnio de Bolívar" (Bolivar's Insomnia), Volpi declares the end of Latin American literature as we know it, saying that that "maker's seal no longer exists." He places Bolaño in the tradition of the Continent, a territory that the Chilean knowingly made use of.

> He is one of the writers who was most aware of the Latin American tradition and measured himself against it. He was also very aware of what he wanted to do in the context of that tradition. He was really very sure of it and that was why his relationship with the world was so strange, there was incredible animosity, incredible violence, but also enormous admiration.
>
> For Bolaño, Cortázar was essential. He was a cult writer for an entire generation, and Bolaño had managed to make himself into a cult writer for another Latin American generation that venerates him with almost the same degree of awe and the same lack of critical distance, which I find dangerous.
>
> Cortázar's *Hopscotch* was a cult novel for an entire generation of Latin American readers and writers in the same way that *The Savage Detectives* is today. Over time, the reaction against *Hopscotch* from that same generation was very violent, and one can anticipate an equally violent reaction against *The Savage Detectives*. In fact, it may have already begun.

In fact, I'm going to say something that Bolaño's fans will find unforgivable: I don't like Bolaño's short stories. I'd even go so far as to say that Bolaño wasn't a very good story writer, although he did write a couple of memorable ones. I confess that I always had the impression that Bolaño's stories, like his poems in some ways, were often sketches or notes for longer texts, for the mid-length pieces he wrote so well and the long texts of which he was a master. That's why it seems to me to be a mistake to publish the texts he didn't want published, and also the fragments, stories, and truncated poems, a patchwork that does nothing to enhance his greatness, and even diminishes it a little, as though every line he ever wrote were a miracle or some kind of votive offering.[1]

In Jorge Volpi's view, Roberto Bolaño never felt close to his own generation of Latin American writers. Neither does he think that he was part of the Spanish generation "which he would have liked to have been part of, but the Spanish didn't pay him any attention at the time."

Borges was always present, however. "I think that Borges was very important to him as a writer, but he never spoke as much about Borges as he did about other, far less important writers," Volpi says.

Bolaño published *The Savage Detectives* in 1998, and the following year *In Search of Klingsor* by Jorge Volpi came out. The two writers inevitably came in contact while promoting their novels. In an interview, Bolaño spoke about Volpi's book, especially a passage he liked very much. News of this reached Volpi.

They met for the first time at the Santiago de Chile Book Fair.

VOLPI: He wasn't a famous writer at all at the time. He went to his home country ready to cause a fuss with his colleagues and compatriots, so perhaps that was why we were able to meet without the animosity, the need to be provocative, which he felt with the Chileans.

His conversation was fascinating for its brilliance, for its erudition, for its unconventionality, the way he forever avoided cliché, the way he uncovered secret connections between authors you would never have thought had anything in common, and that controversial drive that kept him going until his final days ...

A strong memory I have of my relationship with Roberto occurred in Paris. We met there several times.[2] He was traveling to promote the translations of his books—apparently it was the first place where he started to have major critical success—and I worked at the Mexican embassy there at the time. I remember a day we spent together with great fondness. Carolina and their children were there, as were Gonzalo Garcés[3] and Fabienne Bradu[4] ... We spent the whole day together in Paris. If there's one thing I'd like to do with him again it would be that tour. I was showing him things he was interested in in the city, and we kept up a literary conversation for the whole day, going to eat, talking about literature, with him being angry, exultant, funny. It was fantastic.

I think that the focus of his work is fiction. He has some fantastic poems, even some from his time in Mexico, but they are perhaps too much governed by a desire to be rational and also to provoke, to be constantly in conflict with Hispanic American poetic tradition and breaking with it. But he also found stories in his poems that he then turned into fiction.

Volpi thinks that the structures of Bolaño's novels are the result of a manifestly rational instinct and that each has a clear architecture.

"The way he organizes the material, the way each piece is built with an almost musical sensibility and always with enormous ambition, even the brief texts," he says. He thinks that the Bolaño boom was the result of a series of coincidences inextricably linked to the author's early death. First Spanish readers were seduced, followed by Latin American readers, who started to read him eagerly only after *The Savage Detectives*, with a "sentimental fervor." Then he amazed the English-language market, which set him on the global stage.

On the Continent, "for writers of our generation and the next one, his literature contains many of the different paths of the boom and post-boom, or whatever you want to call it, and consolidates an enormous number of fictional possibilities."

VOLPI: Many of us may well hate the poetics of our colleagues, but we coincide in our admiration of Bolaño. In Latin America, I think there is a sense of sentimental and critical affinity that becomes something else when transferred into English.

It's still difficult to explain his current success, like a pop star, especially in the United States. It's been suggested that it might have to do with the reinvention not just of his work but also of his image. I think there's some truth in that, the emphasis English critics have placed on him being a rebel or an addict, which was so controversial. That was never mentioned during his reception in the Hispanic world because it was unimportant. What really mattered was the books.

What Bolaño also had was an ability to represent a faith in literature to the English-speaking world, which had lost it somewhat with all the postmodern games of English literature. Bolaño had this passion for the literary, for how literature can directly influence life, and this placed him in the English-speaking tradition of rebel writers who revolutionize society.

Jorge Volpi says that Roberto Bolaño was the most political writer of recent Latin American generations. He had a very
different political approach to the boom writers: "One could call
his approach almost postpolitical because it isn't ideologically
committed to any one thing, but is still radically political and I
think that that also was of great interest to the English-speaking
world, where he became a cult writer as well as, clearly, a commercial phenomenon."

Forty years after *One Hundred Years of Solitude*, *The Savage
Detectives* repeated the sales and critical success achieved by the
Colombian Gabriel García Márquez. Volpi says, "There is a certain continuity between magical realism and Bolaño's strange,
cynical, radical realism."

What Volpi wants to make clear is that Roberto Bolaño
was in no way a poverty-stricken beggar wandering the streets
of Barcelona. On the contrary: "He lived a middle-class life in
Blanes, very different than the experience of other Hispano-
American immigrants who arrived at more or less the same time
that he started to publish his books. His literature contains a petit
bourgeois obsession with money, which perhaps wasn't true of his
real life."

•   •   •

Adolfo Bioy Casares once wrote: "Doctor Johnson, one of the
most extraordinary critics of writers there ever was, said on one
occasion that 'Only a nincompoop would write for pleasure.' He
wrote out of necessity, for money, and he did it very well."

This sentiment could well apply to Bolaño. Antoni García
Porta, with whom the Chilean cowrote his first novel, *Consejos
de un discípulo de Morrison a un fanático de Joyce* (Advice from a
Disciple of Morrison to a Fan of Joyce), remembers how Bolaño

was very poor when he lived in Calle Tallers in Barcelona: "I suppose that it was the cheapest place he could find. During the winter, Roberto spent his weekends working as a night watchman at a campsite in Castelldefels. He ate, bought notebooks, pens, books, and not much else. In the summer, he went to the campsite for four months, which helped him to save enough money to pay the rent for the rest of the year." Porta remembers that when he did get a little money, he'd bring Bolaño yogurts and cigarettes. They'd smoke and chat.[5]

About money, Bolaño's stepmother recalls: "He didn't have any money when he started to write; his father supported him. León gave him ten pesos every eight days, and this was enough for him to get around, the tram was still around in those days, it charged thirty-five cents and he wouldn't accept more than ten pesos. 'Just take twenty pesos,' my husband said to him, but he'd say he was fine with what he had ... He always said that he wanted to be a great, famous writer and that he wouldn't exchange anything for literature."[6]

Roberto Bolaño wasn't interested in material goods, but his constant mentions of money revealed a dream (a "*guijiro*" dream, as they say in Mexico, to describe impossible dreams) of being able to live off literature without ever having to compromise on his literary projects. His actual livelihood was very different from the romantic image, especially in the Anglo-Saxon imagination, of a writer willing to go hungry and give up everything for his literature.

A more accurate description would be taken from Marguerite Duras in *Writing*: "In life there comes a moment, and I think it is a fatal one that can't be escaped, where you begin to doubt everything: your marriage, friends, especially the couple's friends. Not a child. You never doubt a child ... That makes writing savage. One connects to a prehistoric savagery. We always recognize it, it's that of the forests, as old as time."[7] Bolaño's writing was as savage as the codes he was committed to in his own literature, which wasn't to say that he wouldn't have liked to have a little more money and thus an easier life.

Jorge Volpi believes that "in most of his books, politics is a crucial element; *Nazi Literature in the Americas*, *Distant Star*, and of course *By Night in Chile*.

"In *The Savage Detectives* it might be more elusive, but then it comes back very powerfully in *2666*. Politics is an essential and crucial subject," he adds.

"He asked me a little about Mexico, but not much ... Roberto was preparing an anthology of young Latin American writers. I mean, given that all these texts by Bolaño are coming out, the anthology project ought to be part of it. He got quite far with it until he put it aside to write *2666*. It shows his reading of later generations, or not really later in the case of Alan Pauls, Daniel Seda, or Juan Villoro, whom Bolaño admired so much."

> VOLPI: I must point out that at the time, Bolaño seemed the better contemporary but was also a kind of discovery of ours, and that's what he also valued greatly. He wasn't, as people are now saying, a guru to us. He didn't suddenly choose this or that writer and say nice things about him. At the time he wasn't the firmly established writer he is now. Also, the age difference wasn't that big. The relationship Bolaño maintained with his contemporaries was dialectic.

· · ·

Much has been said about that now legendary gathering in Seville, which turned out to be Roberto Bolaño's last trip. A few weeks later, he'd die in his hospital bed in Barcelona.

"Sevilla Kills Me," a text Roberto wrote about the gathering of Latin American writers, has spread far and wide. Among other things, he wrote: "The river is wide and mighty and its surface is broken by the heads of at least twenty-five writers under fifty, under forty, under thirty. How many will drown? I'd say all of them."[8]

Volpi remembers Seville as a turning point for his contemporaries.

VOLPI: [Seville was the] canonization of Bolaño by my generation and it happened ten days before he died. The memories are vivid because they are also our last. I took a very active part in organizing the gathering together with my publisher at the time, Seix Barral, and the Lara Foundation. We felt that Bolaño had to be there, and also Guillermo Cabrera Infante, who may have been a boom writer, he was at the core of the boom, but he was always very close to younger writers. It was very interesting to see Bolaño and Cabrera Infante, who are both now dead, spending those five days in Seville. We went everywhere together. It was a strange event, without an audience. No one bothered us, and in the day-to-day business I think that Roberto came to realize how important he was. We went out for a walk once, and he bought a copy of *Libération*, which had an article about him. It was a long article, full of praise, and it made him very happy.

All the conference-goers were asked to bring a written text, but Roberto didn't bring anything. He just brought the fragment that has now become so famous: "Sevilla Kills Me."

It seemed more of a statement, trying to anticipate the terrible future more than anything else. It was published as if it were a work of fiction, but very probably it's no more than a quarter of the text he was going to write, just a fragment of the text, a fragment in which he tells jokes and constantly makes fun of what's going on. Some critics have tried to see something

serious in that text, as proof that he went to Seville to make fun
of the other writers, which is what Ignacio Echevarría said. I
radically disagree with that. I firmly believe that that was just
the start of the text and that he was probably going to say more
later on. In the end, he didn't even read it. At his conference he
said: "I wanted to write a text called 'Sevilla Kills Me' but I only
got to write a few paragraphs, so I'm going to read a text I wrote
for another congress,"[9] and he read something else.

Roberto Bolaño is, in Volpi's eyes, something that the Mexican writer has said and written often: the last Latin American
writer.

VOLPI: He truly took on the mantle of being Latin American.
I remember very long conversations with him in which his erudition in Latin American literature was genuinely enormous.
He had really read a huge amount of minor authors from the
nineteenth century and the beginning of the twentieth century
with whom in some way he kept up a dialogue. His own writing
is also essentially Latin American. His fantastic work is perhaps
his great answer to all the novels of the boom, *The Green House*,
Terra Nostra, and *One Hundred Years of Solitude*.

14

Pretty Stubborn with Women

They were all the women of his life—You finally have a face!—The delicate cigarettes—Poetic fainting in the plaza—The certainty of Roberto's love—The same birthday as Saddam Hussein—Don't let me die of hunger—I never saw him go inside—There's plenty more women—The damn notes—Even if you're crying out in pain

Those who knew Bolaño describe him as a man whom women found attractive, even though he was no pretty boy, having lost his teeth at an early age, like Martin Amis and Vladimir Nabokov.

His father, León, saw him as a seductive, charismatic man: "When I went to Spain in 2002, he introduced me to his wife, although I don't know if she really was his wife, because he was pretty saucy with the ladies. He liked girls a lot.

"In Mexico, he went everywhere with a girl," his father remembers. "She was the daughter of a foreigner and a writer like him. He took her to Cuernavaca and they spent about a month together, until the girl's mother came to get her. Roberto came to me one night to ask me to go with him to get her things from Cuernavaca. 'She left me. They came to get her,' he said."

He was an archetypal romantic. In the tradition of courtly love, he was more in love with the idea of love than with the woman. Never-ending letters, occasionally repeated over time, were the preferred form of approach for the born seducer, an example of his emotional need to be the center of attention. He would succumb to the burning flame of romantic disappointment so as to make himself the victim, while on other occasions he might take on the role of hero, to sacrifice himself, brandishing the banner of love as though it were his alone to bear.

Ponç Puigdevall says it well: love is not one of the foundations of Bolaño's literature—sex is. He doesn't seem to have been a man who loved women, a great lover, but rather an eternal child who, in search of constant adventure, would dance on the precipice of an erupting volcano before fleeing just in time but not without being hurt in the process.

What will certainly surprise many when the whole archive of the correspondence is opened up, if all the people who received his letters make them available to the public, will be the number of repeated phrases and the number of anecdotes told in exactly the same way to different recipients. As his first editor, Juan Pascoe, says, Bolaño wrote for posterity, for the world, not for a specific person. He seems to have been the same way when it came to romance.

The man who bequeathed his life and legacy to just one woman, Carolina López, the mother of his children, brings to mind Peter Sellars. The actor was absurdly childish in his romantic affairs, and after dying from a heart attack at fifty-three years of age, he was found to have a single photograph in his pocket: that of his first wife, the mother of his first two children.

It is interesting to note that all the women interviewed for this book who had a close relationship with Bolaño at one time or another remember him with that air of lost love. They are themselves lost in a somewhat diffuse but recurring atmosphere: the notion of what might have been but wasn't, and what certainly wasn't.

Like all seducers, Bolaño doesn't escape the crude cliché of the great, charming conqueror of women who tells them what they want to hear. This was a pattern that was repeated with his friendships.

Many people believe themselves to have been friends of Bolaño's, and the writer treated them all as such at one time or another, making them feel the objects of his dearest affection. In Mexico, the popular concept "*mero mero*" is used to describe the "top dog" of an organization, or the pinnacle of a person's affection. Bolaño seems to have had few mero meros in his heart: his children primarily; his mother, Victoria Ávalos; his wife, Carolina López; and his sister, María Salomé.

Of course, there was also the lost friend, perhaps the alter ego who lived life to an extreme that the writer could never have experienced for himself, but whom he nonetheless saw as a grand utopian failure: Mario Santiago Papasquiaro.

On the other hand, it wouldn't be surprising, once his correspondence is released, if we were also to see Roberto only taking vicarious enjoyment in romantic affairs.

He might have also been a voyeur, bearing witness to himself in various ways: He didn't drink yet was a master at recounting the torments of alcoholism. He had never been to the north of Mexico and yet was able to write—and even foretell—the hell of Ciudad Juárez, its story multiplied a hundred times over in so many other areas of poor, bloody Mexico.

Bolaño lived so briefly but so intensely that his life is often confused with his books. Unfortunately, it is his literature that bears the *carotin* (another Mexican phrase, roughly meaning "stamp" or "proof") of his existence. Life for this brilliant storyteller was in fact much more monotonous, predictable, and even boring than he liked to admit, and many of his loves, friends, and interests became interesting only because he included them in his fantastic literary universe.

Getting back to women, many accounts describe a man who put feelers out everywhere—who loved to be in correspondence with women—but allowed himself to be tied down only to the protective harbor of his home and the arms of the woman who lived with him for twenty years. This was the woman to whom he left all responsibility for his work, and to whom he dedicated his most important books, the woman he rarely failed to mention in his interviews.

Although in his final years Roberto Bolaño appeared to spend

much time with Carmen Pérez de Vega, there is no doubt of the
continuing importance of his wife. She was the woman he says
he seduced after cooking her rice in every different way imagin-
able, and with whom he created the most important people in his
life: his son and daughter.

Did women find him attractive? Did he preserve the charming spark of humor that had made so many girls sigh in his
youth?

The journalist and writer Paola Tinoco, the current representative of the publisher Anagrama in Mexico, met Roberto Bolaño
in 2002. She was accompanying one of his best friends, the writer
Sergio González Rodríguez,[1] who doesn't like to travel alone, to
his launch of *Huesos en el desierto* (Bones in the Desert). The book,
published by Anagrama in 2001, is a gripping account of the crimes
against women in Ciudad Juárez, and was one of the works that
most influenced Bolaño when writing *2666*.[2] For a few months
before they met in person at the launch, Bolaño and González
Rodríguez exchanged a profuse amount of letters and e-mails.

Here is my interview with Tinoco.

MARISTAIN: *What was it like when you first met?*

TINOCO: It was chaos, because he invited us to dinner in Blanes
and we were in Barcelona. We thought that the trains in the sur-
rounding area were as frequent as the urban ones. So we got on
the first that came by. It said "BLANES" but went in the other
direction. We got there three hours late. When we got off the
train we called him on his cell phone, and he offered to come and
pick us up from the corner we were on with his son. For some
reason we decided to change the corner we were on, and when
he got there he couldn't find us, and we spent another hour
looking for each other. We were starving. As was to be expected,

he and his family had already eaten. Finally, we found each other and he invited us to have a drink at home. On a completely empty stomach! We hadn't even had breakfast! Half an hour later, we finally confessed that we were half dead, and Carolina very kindly made us some bruschetta … And that was our meal with Bolaño.

MARISTAIN: *What do you remember about his house?*

TINOCO: That there were books everywhere, including on the highest shelves, where I couldn't reach but he could. It was also very dark.

MARISTAIN: *And what was he like?*

TINOCO: Well, he wasn't a particularly attractive man, but he had overwhelming charm. There was something about the way he treated women that definitely caught your attention. His charm, I think, consisted of challenging you, throwing down the gauntlet. He asked you things like: "And how about you? What have you read?" Or he'd ask you about the Mexican women you supposedly read as a girl. I asked him: "Why do you think that I read women's literature?" And he answered: "What? Mexico has women like Margo Glantz and Carmen Boullosa." I said that I read them most of all, and we laughed.

MARISTAIN: *How did the meeting between him and Sergio go?*

TINOCO: "You finally have a face!" Roberto said to Sergio. At one point they started to talk about what they were both writing at the time, and that was when Sergio found out that he was a character in *2666*. "I'm writing the longest novel of my life," Bolaño said. It wasn't the first time for Sergio, he had already been a character in a novel by Javier Marías,[3] but he was very happy.

MARISTAIN: *And when did you see Roberto again?*

TINOCO: The second time I saw him was in Barcelona, in a Japanese restaurant. He came with [his friend Carmen Pérez de Vega], and I was presented with a much more friendly man who smiled a lot more ... He was beaming, very sparkly, very alive. He was trying not to smoke, but I tempted him a lot. I smoked at the time and had brought Delicados, which had been his cigarettes when he lived in Mexico. I remember him as a man who wanted to seem tough but who had a very sweet side. I know it's very silly to say this, but that's what I most remember about him.

MARISTAIN: *How do Roberto Bolaño's books sell in Mexico?*

TINOCO: His book sales exploded after his death. Before he died, only *The Savage Detectives* sold well, but then all the others started to as well. *2666* broke Anagrama's records for the country. Until Bolaño, only Paul Auster and Alessandro Baricco sold much in Mexico.

MARISTAIN: *How do you view Roberto's work after his death?*

TINOCO: I think that what Roberto wanted to say with his books has already been said. My opinion is that everything that came out after *2666*, including *The Unknown University*, is stuff that Bolaño didn't want people to read. They're texts that he didn't approve of. Other people do, maybe people he trusted greatly, I don't doubt it, but the author is the best judge of whether things should be published or not.

MARISTAIN: *When did you hear that Roberto Bolaño was about to die?*

TINOCO: When I came back from my last trip to Barcelona. I remember having read a piece in which he said that he found it very amusing to be fainting poetically in plazas. He said it as a joke and so that's how I took it, but then I heard that he fainted because he was very sick, was on a waiting list for a liver transplant that kept being delayed because he was a smoker. He tried to smoke less—I can bear testimony to that—but he still smoked a lot. A memory that moved me at the time was Sergio bringing him a packet of La Habana Coffee and Roberto smelling the coffee at length with a lot of nostalgia and a certain melancholy, because he couldn't drink coffee anymore. Every Thursday, he went to Barcelona to see the doctor and Carmen, who seemed to be part of the treatment. Roberto's mood changed completely when he was with Carmen. His eyes lit up when she was around, he made jokes, messed around ... Carmen is a very pretty woman, with the kind of face that declares she owes nothing to nobody.

● ● ●

An important woman in Roberto Bolaño's life was Paloma Díaz, his great friend from childhood in Mexico. She describes herself as a "Mexican painter with Oaxacan and Yucateca roots," and has said that she wouldn't at all mind having a little luck but utterly deplores fame.

Paloma was surprised by Roberto's death. She had just renewed her friendship with the writer, whom she had met in 1976. She belonged to the Suma group, an artistic movement that worked with the Infrarealists.

"I didn't have an intellectual or artistic relationship with him. Roberto was a friend, a very generous person who had the same birthday as me [April 28]," she says. "He lived in a very modest house on the way to Villa. Once, I don't know what we were doing at his house but he took his passport out from under his bed, a little cot, to show me that he wasn't joking, that we really had been born on the same day.[4] So we became like brother and sister. We shared a birthday with Saddam Hussein."

To Paloma, Roberto was always "a great romantic." She did not drink, take drugs, or smoke at the time, and felt obliged to draw in secret, "because I belonged to a conceptual group for whom drawing was complete heresy. Roberto, in contrast, really liked my drawings."

She remembers that Bolaño said that he didn't want to be a "great writer" but wrote "because he had no alternative ... He never stopped writing, he was always carrying around crumpled pieces of paper. When we wrote to each other, his letters made me laugh a lot, because they're illustrated; he also liked to draw."

Bolaño very much liked the Costa Rican poet Ninfa Santos,[5] Paloma's grandmother, to whom he immediately took a liking and never forgot to greet in his letters.

Paloma and Roberto shared a relationship of sibling love, "which doesn't very often occur between real siblings," she says, and the artist often went to visit him in Barcelona. The visits were pleasurable, and Bolaño committed his scarce time to them, even though "he was always in the middle of some tumultuous love affair." Paloma also saw Bruno Montané on those trips, as well as his girlfriend Inma, with whom she was great friends. Bolaño would write to Díaz, asking to pass on kisses to her grandmother, and to get gossip from their Mexico days and mutual friends.[6] "Of course, he was always starving because he didn't eat anything and just smoked all the time. It was part, I think, of a very romantic vision in which he had to keep on struggling," says Paloma.

The Roberto Bolaño that Paloma Díaz knew "was a kitten compared to Mario Santiago, who we were terrified of. He was sweet. Also, our relationship was just between him and me; I didn't accompany them on their escapades. Roberto was a very gentle and affectionate person. Anyone would have been his friend. They would be today, too, if he were still alive. Roberto didn't break bonds of friendship."

In perhaps his most significant act of friendship, Bolaño dedicated a poem—"Olor a plástico quemado" (Smell of Burning Plastic)—to Díaz.

DÍAZ: Roberto read that poem to me in his room and I died of emotion. I was eighteen or nineteen at the time, and of course I had never had a poem dedicated to me in my life. I did get a little nervous, because I felt, at heart, that he was teasing me, but I liked the poem. It's still here. Roberto took great care of me. I had fallen into that world of frenetic poets and painters who were a kind of missing link, and it all scared me. Roberto always made sure that they didn't make fun of me, that they didn't mess around with me, and I feel great affection and gratitude toward him because of it.

When I met Roberto, I had just finished school in Rome, Italy. I got to Mexico thinking about entering the National School of the Plastic Arts, that I was going to be a painter and all that. But it turned out that they didn't accept my application and that no one in Mexico painted or drew anymore. Everyone was doing very conceptual things, which wasn't really for me. But I joined the urban art movement and it was an incredible experience. I also became part of a Mexico City that was beautiful but also terrifying. All of us spent all our time on the street. At La

Habana Café, going from action to action, from house to house. It was a wonderful time, very magical and also very terrible.

I was amazed when I heard some people say that Roberto might have died because of problems with heroin. I never saw him take anything. I mean, he was crazy, but he just smoked. It really annoys me to hear people talk about his supposed drug addiction, because not in Mexico or Spain, where I saw him several times, did Roberto have anything to do with anything like that.

· · ·

Carla Rippey met Roberto Bolaño in the Mexico of the 1970s. The American artist, who is portrayed in *The Savage Detectives* as Catalina O'Hara, lived in Chile for a time and has lived in Mexico since 1985.

Her memories of Bolaño are moving. He was a close friend. When the writer left for Spain she kept up a regular correspondence with him. At sixty-three years old, she's still a very beautiful woman, and her artistic activity is intense and unstoppable.

MARISTAIN: *Is Roberto a ghost?*

RIPPEY: He's become a ghost, although to me he was a ghost since long before his physical disappearance, because I didn't see him for twenty-seven years. When he was twenty-three and I was twenty-five, I went with him to the airport in Mexico City, with my son Luciano, whom Roberto adored, and my son Andrés in my arms. That was when I met his father, who had also gone to say goodbye to him at the airport. I already knew his mother. I had met her in an apartment on Calle Londres, in the Rosa area, where she lived for a while with her daughter, María Salomé.

MARISTAIN: *And did the young man you knew give any inkling of the literary phenomenon he would become today?*

RIPPEY: I was completely convinced of it. As early as 1995, more or less, I started to think: "How strange, Roberto isn't famous yet!" I had the privilege of getting many letters from him, and I would have got many more if I had been a better letter writer. A moment came when I stopped answering, and so communication was broken off. In 1994, I got a very long letter from him, answering a package I had sent him containing my exhibition catalogs. Then I lost track of him and after a few years I sought him out again. I was reluctant to write to his P.O. box; I didn't even know if he still had it. The year he died, I started to look for him over the Internet and contacted a journalist who had interviewed him in Chile. I sent an e-mail to the journalist, called Felipe, asking him to give my e-mail address to Roberto.

MARISTAIN: *What was Roberto's literature like when you were, as you often say, his early reader?*

RIPPEY: First, I say that because of the amazing quality of his letters, which all deserve to be published. His poems were also fantastic. The other person in the group Roberto believed to be better than him was Mario Santiago, of course. In a conversation I had with Roberto a month before he died, he told me that he'd have liked to have the time to bring out a collection of Mario's work.

MARISTAIN: *Was he an affectionate person?*

RIPPEY: Yes, with his friends. With Mario, Bruno Montané, me, my children, my ex-husband. With the Infrarealists, in contrast, his relationships were much more stressful, less intimate. He was very passionate about the people he really cared about. I have a letter from him in which he says that he saw my ex-husband[7] on television in Spain and he instinctively wanted to hug the television.

MARISTAIN: *What did you feel when you read* The Savage Detectives?

RIPPEY: The first thing anyone who knew Roberto did was look through the novel to find the parts that featured us. It must have been a very powerful experience for the Larrosa sisters [Mara and Vara], who are major characters[8] in the first part. Especially to find oneself portrayed in a way that didn't quite reflect reality. In my case, it's true that I had a baby, and that I got divorced soon afterward, although Roberto didn't witness that, as I was still with my husband when he left Mexico. When we separated, I told Roberto all about it in my letters. What wasn't true was that there were lots of parties at my house. Neither does my political activism feature, and I was very intensely involved at the time. My ex-husband and I were in Chile when the Pinochet coup happened, and I had been a feminist activist in Boston ...

MARISTAIN: *Did you talk about the situation in Chile or Mexico?*

RIPPEY: The truth is that the only thing that we cared about at the time was that we got on well and were interested in the same kinds of things: art, what we wanted to do in life ...

MARISTAIN: *Why do you think he never wanted to go back to Mexico?*

RIPPEY: Obviously Roberto built a personal territory in Mexico, which was very important for his literature, and I think that he wanted to keep it that way. When I say that, I think about what happened to me in Xalapa, a place where I lived for five years because I married a guy from there. When I went back, the first thing I felt was a very powerful sensation of everything closing in on me all at once, but on subsequent trips the memories faded. I get the impression that if Roberto had gone back to Mexico, his literary Mexico would have ceased to exist.

MARISTAIN: *Only that way could he write* The Savage Detectives, *which is considered by many to be the great contemporary Mexican novel...*

RIPPEY: To me *The Savage Detectives* was his great private joke with Mario Santiago. I think that Roberto thought that his great novel was *2666*. At least that's what he implies in a letter from 1994, when he started to write it. *The Savage Detectives* ... was the long journey of his youth. Mexico City was a sacred place to him. It came out in his letters and he discussed it a little with me. He said that he lived in a village, that he had grown up in a village, that he wasn't a man for big cities, but in the end ...

MARISTAIN: *Which do you think is his best book?*

RIPPEY: *2666*, even though it's so terrible. Although I think that one of the things I like most about Roberto is that even when he writes about the most terrible things, he always finds a twist to give the reader a lift. *2666* isn't his most fun or playful work, but the dialogues between the three professors are very funny.

MARISTAIN: *Was he disciplined in his writing?*

RIPPEY: Yes, absolutely, he wrote all the time. He smoked, wrote, smoked, and wrote letters, that was all Roberto did.

MARISTAIN: *Did he tell you about his disease?*

RIPPEY: In his last letter from 1995, he said to me: "Write to me, so I can tell you a lot more and also about diseases." But he didn't mention it explicitly. If he had said something I would definitely have answered immediately. The truth is that it was difficult for me to write to Bolaño. I loved him a lot and if I wrote to him often, it began to interfere with my daily life, because I don't have the capacity he had to separate the two areas. I would have started to fall in love with him, which would have been terrible because there was no way I was going to go to Spain or anything like that. I think that that was why I chose to distance myself.

MARISTAIN: *Do you feel guilty about that?*

RIPPEY: Very guilty, of course. And more than anything now that I have lost him. I found out about his illness through the newspapers. I contacted him over the Internet when he was very sick, three or four months before the end. I think that that made the loss more bearable, though it was obviously a huge blow. Before he died, we spoke for an hour on the telephone. It was very difficult to get in touch because he never found me, and when I wanted to call him I didn't have his number. He said that because of the fans he didn't have a telephone line ... In the final few days, he was very concerned with finding Lisa, the girlfriend he had been with in Mexico. He wanted to reconcile with her, as he had treated her very badly. So I spoke to Lisa, but she wanted nothing to do with him; she said that her relationship with Roberto was in the past. On that phone call he told me that he took his daughter to the beach and came back home exhausted, devoid of strength. When I spoke to him, he hadn't completely resigned himself to dying. His blood type made the transplant even more difficult. He was third in line when he died. Maybe he would have managed it—who knows? He was very worried about the convalescence; how would his family live after the transplant?

MARISTAIN: *Was he happy when he wrote?*

RIPPEY: I don't think that he was himself if he wasn't writing. In a letter he told me that he had been diagnosed as having a bipolar disorder. I don't know if he did really, but he was a man of extreme character and I think that the writing accelerated a lot when he knew he was close to death. We had a very special relationship. He had close relationships with my brother-in-law Juan Pascoe, who was his first publisher, and my ex-husband, but they were much more formal. I suppose that the fact that he was a man and I was a woman made the relationship even more intense and also explained why I cut it off eventually. How can you keep up such an intense relationship over a long distance?

MARISTAIN: *Were you in love with Roberto Bolaño?*

RIPPEY: Not exactly. Well, when we were together it wouldn't have occurred to me, because I was very much in love with my husband. I considered it some time later, but he had gone to Spain. Roberto was great, I loved being with him. When I separated, the first thing I thought was what a pity it was that Roberto wasn't in Mexico. My brother-in-law always said "your beloved Roberto," but I also know that he treated the people he loved as though he were in love. He fell in love with his friends, not just his girlfriends. He treated Mario Santiago, for example, like a lover. One also has to acknowledge that it was Roberto's human qualities that allowed him to be such a good writer. You can't separate the two with him. Of course there are people, like Isabel Allende, who think that Roberto was a son of a bitch, but I didn't see his terrible side. I once saw his depressive side, but never his terrible, ferocious one.

MARISTAIN: *He wasn't at all handsome, but he was very seductive . . .*

RIPPEY: Who told you that he wasn't handsome? He was extremely handsome, of course.

MARISTAIN: *Did you meet Carolina, his wife?*

RIPPEY: No, because when we got back in contact in '94 or '95, he had separated. I had some correspondence with Carmen, who seems to me to be very discreet. She never wanted to cause any problems with his family; she never wanted to take center stage.

MARISTAIN: *If you were to write to him now, what would your letter say?*

RIPPEY: I'd laugh a lot in it and I'd make him laugh about everything that's happening with his public image after his death. Although, really, I think that he was aware of how important he would become after his death. The fame that surrounds him now had started when he was still alive, so I think that he's controlling everything we're doing with him from up there. I remember that in one of the last telephone conversations we had he told me how no one had wanted to tell him that Mario Santiago had died. He said that eventually it was Juan Villoro who worked up the courage to tell him, about two months after it happened. I'm like

Catalina O'Hara in *The Savage Detectives*, a shrill gringa crybaby, and I cried a lot, a lot, when I heard that Roberto had died.

• • •

Roberto Bolaño says in his last interview that he suffered deeply from love the first time. "Then I learned to have a bit more of a sense of humor about it." He also said that he had thought about killing himself several times in his life and that "occasionally I survived precisely because I knew I could kill myself if things got any worse."

Suffering deeply for love and wishing one's own death were two things that seemed closely linked when the first great love of his life, Lisa, obeyed her mother and left the young writer's house in Guadalupe Tepeyac, a major traumatic event of his childhood, as mentioned earlier.

According to Irene, Bolaño's stepmother: "Roberto took Lisa, his girlfriend, to live in that room. They spent barely a month and a few days there together before Lisa's mother came to get her and told her to leave. Roberto was very downhearted, very sad. Once, I don't know why, but I came back early from work and knocked on his door because I heard a groaning, but he didn't open it. So I went inside and he was lying on the bed, raving, even frothing at the mouth." Irene ran off to look for help from a clinic nearby, where they "pumped his stomach because he had taken a lot of pills." Back at home, Roberto and his father had a conversation behind closed doors. " 'Apparently he poisoned himself over a woman—there's plenty more women,' was what León said to me," recalls Irene.

"They loved each other, but her mother separated them. 'What do you want with a writer who has nothing?' she said. He was very upset. He didn't sleep, he was very much in love and thought about killing himself. I convinced him that killing your-self over a woman was stupid," says León Bolaño.

"She was the girl he should have married. She was charming, a first-class writer. To me she was like a second daughter. But only they know what happened and you can't get involved," said Roberto's mother.[9]

The mark that Lisa left on Bolaño's life was deep, to the extent that, as the artist Carla Rippey says, in one of her last telephone conversations with the writer, he said that he wanted to contact his childhood girlfriend (portrayed in *The Savage Detectives* as Laura Jáuregui) "to reconcile because he had treated her very badly."

Lisa's lips were one of Roberto's clearest Latin American memories, he told me in his last interview. The girl, furthermore, is constantly evoked in Bolaño's work, as in the poems "Lisa" and "El recuerdo de Lisa" (The Memory of Lisa).

Today Lisa is a prestigious researcher—she doesn't want to talk about Roberto Bolaño.

•   •   •

In Blanes, Roberto made friends with Marta Matas, a young, beautiful woman who "adopted" the writer on some of his summer visits before he settled in the pretty Catalan seaside town with his new wife.

Marta, who worked as a nanny in the 1980s, accompanied one of her charges to Victoria Ávalos's accessories store, where Roberto was employed. Bolaño, who Marta says "never let an opportunity to speak to a girl pass him by," immediately tried to strike up a conversation.

The store sold normal things, the kind that you see in a lot of other stores, and Roberto wasn't a very committed salesman; he was distracted a lot of the time.

Marta remembers Bolaño as someone who was "charming, very friendly, and we quickly became close friends." He also had "a well-developed feminine side," which allowed a very open level of intimacy in the friendship.

"It might not be that easy to live with him, to see him every day, I don't know, but if you just saw him for a chat and spent some time together, it was very easy and pleasant to be with him," she remembers. "He said that he loved to listen, but the truth is that with his hoarse voice and eternal cigarette between his fingers, talking was what he liked to do best."

In terms of romance, Bolaño was convinced that you had to try a Latin American "because they were the best." This was the main piece of advice he gave to female friends like Marta.

MATAS: He came to my house quite a lot, because he was very lonely for a time. Once, when I visited the hospital to see a relative, he had been admitted there too. He came to see me regularly. He looked and looked until he found me … I really miss him.

I saw him go through tough times financially. He was very poor and didn't have many friends. Of the few friends he had in Blanes, many are now dead. This town has a whole generation lost to drugs, and Roberto made friends with the addicts. He had a weakness for people going through a bad time.

His son, Lautaro, was everything to him, especially after the disease started to get worse. He spent every moment he could with him, swimming, going to the beach, playing those war games.[10]

Before I met Roberto, my favorite writer was Javier Marías. So when he started to get published, I was happy because he'd be on my bookshelf next to Marías, who was an author he admired a lot.

If he was low on money or food, he didn't ask, he just announced that he was coming to have dinner at my house that night. He did that for Christmas one year when he was alone and invited himself. I was there with my whole family and Roberto turned up. We ended up playing a trivia game after the toast.

Sometimes it annoyed me that he thought he knew everything. I would say: "So what?" He once told me that he was the intellectual around here. Of course he said that when he started to get published; he wouldn't have said so before. Roberto changed. Maybe because the change was inevitable, but things weren't the same after he started to win recognition. When he became a literary figure, he started to have lots of people around him all the time.

I miss him a lot now that he has died, but really I started to miss him before, when he became famous. I knew that the distance that came between him and the people he used to spend time with was a bad thing, but I thought it was normal, that's what happens when you become important.

Apart from his amorous flings, which took a lot out of him, Roberto lived a quiet life in Blanes. A normal middle-class life. He didn't take drugs or drink alcohol. His habits were healthy, except for the smoking, of course. He fell in love a lot and the affairs didn't last long. I think that he was more in love with the idea of love than any woman in particular.

He didn't like to lend people his books, especially not when they got marks on them. He once asked me to give him a book by Italo Calvino because he said that it was missing from his library, and given how important his library was to him, he felt I had to give it to him. Of course I didn't, and he got a little annoyed.

Sometimes he had to go to the doctor and he took a lot of

pills, but I don't think he knew that his disease was so serious. I, of course, never thought that Roberto would die of it.

He was certainly thin, but he had a belly. He was always more or less the same, until one day a friend told me that she'd heard on the news that Roberto had died. I still can't believe it, sometimes I think that he's gone on a trip and will be back soon. I looked to see where the funeral was going to be held and went to Barcelona. At the funeral I had a horrible experience— I couldn't see him and I'd rather not speak about it.

Now, when I hear all these people talking about Roberto, I don't recognize him. There's a lot of noise about his public figure, and sometimes I think that they're talking about someone else. People have confused his work with his life, with his actual experiences. I know that he wrote a very complex body of work, but his life, at least here, was very simple. A writer is a storyteller, but that doesn't mean that those stories happened to him.

· · ·

Nearly all the memories of Victoria Ávalos, Roberto's mother, are pleasant: the interviews collected in this book attest to this. The writer's friends and girlfriends remember her as a very nice, open woman without any prejudices. They especially remember that she was very cultured.

Bolaño was without a doubt a mother's boy. She was a math teacher who had trouble educating her son in his early childhood. "I didn't know what to do," she said to the Chilean Patricio Jara in a radio interview. "Once, we were walking in Valparaíso, he was three, and we suddenly passed the Velarde cinema. He looked at the signs and started to read out the name of the cinema. At first I thought that he was doing it by memory, but he was reading. It shocked me so much that I took him to the doctor. They said that

I had to take his books away because it was dangerous, he might get stuck in a certain age. The truth was that he was a very intelligent boy."

Distant Star, one the most critically acclaimed books after *The Savage Detectives* and *2666*, was dedicated to Victoria Ávalos, the only woman who was ever able to calm Roberto down, according to his childhood friends.

Victoria, who died of respiratory failure in 2008 at eighty-one years old, in the Catalan town of Figueras, where she lived, praised her son for the generosity with which he "rescued the young addicts from the beach" in Blanes and for, especially, his enormous goodwill. "He was a very lovely person, he liked everyone."

She recalls that Roberto as a child "was playful, he liked to play cowboys, jump around, ride a bicycle. He was very close to his friends. He was a kind of Robin Hood to them: he was always giving them presents. And later on, when he was older, he worried a lot about his friends and also about young people."[11]

Against her husband's will, Victoria supported her son in his wish to dedicate himself completely to literature, and always trusted in his talent. Her influence wasn't just decisive in his literary formation but also because she was there whenever he needed her.

"I don't like it when people say that he was extremely poor. The truth is that he never wanted for anything, it was just that he wanted to take care of everything himself—and the thing is that he always managed it."

•   •   •

Carolina López is Roberto Bolaño's widow. She was married to him for twenty years. She is now in her fifties, very attractive and discreet. She has given very few interviews since the death of her husband, the father of their two children.

They met in Gerona in 1981, when Bolaño was very young and very poor, with a susceptibility to depression. They married in 1985 and were always together in some way until his death, although almost every account states that they had periods of seperation starting in 1994.[12] "He was a man who listened a lot and who got into relationships very deeply, overwhelmingly so," López told her interviewer Erik Haasnoot.[13] "He was very talkative and spoke to anyone he came across. His first friendships were with fishermen and waiters; his literary friends came later."

In a 1998 interview, Bolaño said: "Each of us lives in our own house and we get on much better like that. We've been together for seventeen years, and I recommend it completely because my wife is basically my friend. So there is absolute respect for each other's freedom."

The couple started out living in Blanes so that Roberto could work in Victoria's accessories store. Shortly afterward, López got a bureaucratic post with the municipality, through which she was essentially able to maintain the family.

In an interview with the journalist Josep Massot for the Spanish newspaper *La Vanguardia*, she remembers her husband as a passionate person who was unable to forgive disloyalty and who liked games of strategy. She insists on dispelling the myth about Bolaño being a drug addict or being a writer who lived on literary awards.

Meanwhile, López is the sole administrator of the author's archive, which she described in the interview mentioned above: "When Roberto died, we found boxes with an incredible number of manuscripts, notes, projects, especially poetry, typed documents ... A lot of that material is typed on a typewriter so we were able to date it, because in 1993 he bought an electronic typewriter and in 1995 we got a computer. There are also the computer files and a lot of printed pages that Roberto hadn't saved on a disk or on the hard disk. We've started the process of classifying all the material and done an initial read. We are in the research phase."

•   •   •

María Salomé Bolaño, the author's sister, doesn't like speaking in public. She is very introverted, timid, and even curt. However, she made an exception at the naming ceremony for Carrer de Roberto Bolaño in Gerona, which she attended with her husband and son.

"Yes, he was a very well-loved brother, but also a brother who used to infuriate me," admits María, whom he used to call "Me."

During the naming ceremony, María Salomé said that as she was clearing out her mother's apartment after Victoria died, among the many papers by Roberto she found was one that contained a twelve-point list of advice. The discovery was a great joy for her, bringing her closer to her brother at a difficult time. Among the advice included was to "be loving to yourself and others"; to "learn to keep seeing the beauty of living things even if you're crying out in pain"; and to always keep sight of "silence, laughter, and trust."

15

Final Days

Put a lot of humor into it. Take care of the myth—Seductive as Arturo Belano—Dinner—Locked in the Botanical Gardens in Blanes—Do you think he could be the murderer?—Austere and an epicure—A lot of accidents happen during Easter week—A battle of giants—Calm, dignified, and elegant—A man-work—Roberto has died

"Put a lot of humor into it. Take care of the myth," the Catalan Carmen Pérez de Vega, Roberto Bolaño's companion during the final years of his life, writes in an e-mail.

A woman of undeniable beauty, Carmen Pérez de Vega was an essential witness to the writer's life and without a doubt played an important role in it, as Ignacio Echevarría, one of the people who knew Roberto's work the best, attests.

She has, however, become a taboo figure in discussions of Bolaño's biography, practically reduced to the status of a ghost— some even deny she had any kind of relationship with Bolaño at all. It is difficult to get Carmen Pérez de Vega to speak about her relationship with the author's widow, Carolina López.

That said, there is clearly a dispute between Carmen Pérez de Vega, the writer's companion, and Carolina López, the mother of Bolaño's children: mentions of Pérez de Vega have been deleted from new editions of Bolaño's books, including the dedication to her of "Álvaro Rousselot's Journey" in *The Insufferable Gaucho.*

The entire story has become somewhat tedious and has nothing to do with appreciating Bolaño's work, which is essentially all that matters. It is a symptom of something the writer almost certainly didn't anticipate, never having imagined (or wished, most likely) that his legacy and public figure would become such a phenomenon.

In the following interview, which took place on the Rambla in Barcelona, Pérez de Vega, a fascinating woman of remarkable intelligence and sensitivity, tells her version of history; Bolaño's final night, an adventure in a small car racing against the clock in a vain attempt to save the man she cared deeply about.

During the conversation, a young man stole the cell phones that were lying on the table. During my other meeting with Pérez de Vega, we witnessed a collision between a car and a motorcyclist. The latter ended up on the hood of the car. "They're signs from Bolaño," we said to each other.

MARISTAIN: *What was Roberto like?*

PÉREZ DE VEGA: He was sweet. A really complex person. Actually, I've never really sat down to think about what Roberto was like. Strangely, I don't think about it much. I mean, I've thought about it now and again but not as much as one might think. I don't know how much I care either … He was a very intelligent person, he was loyal, he greatly valued friendship and respect. He was a teacher. Sometimes he was a harsh teacher, but I think that he would have been a good schoolteacher, maybe he got that from his mother. I learned many things from him, and I always say that he was one of the people who was best able to make me believe in myself. Roberto had a leader's temperament, he was constantly trying to promote his theories and get people to follow him, which is why he was also very stubborn. Sometimes it wasn't easy to make him see reason or change his mind. I always make clear that when I met him, Roberto was a certain age and he was sick. Over time, as is to be expected, his character became less brusque, although in essence he was always someone who found it hard to admit that you might be right about something. Toward the end he would concede: "Well, maybe you're right …" To him that was a big concession.

MARISTAIN: *Was he, as people say, a charming person?*

PÉREZ DE VEGA: He could be. I think that in essence he was a seductive person, there was a kind of mystery about him that's difficult to define. His literature is enthralling in part because he is reflected in seductive alter egos like Arturo Belano, although I think that Roberto is also reflected in others, and men and women tend to fall in love with them.

MARISTAIN: *Was he the kind of person who always needed to be the center of attention in a group?*

PÉREZ DE VEGA: It depended. I think that we all have a vain side and like to be the center of something. I don't consider myself a vain person, but I can give you an example from yesterday [referring to the naming ceremony for Carrer de Roberto Bolaño in Gerona, an event that involved Patti Smith, Ignacio Echevarría, Jorge Herralde, and María Salomé Bolaño, the author's sister], when everyone was saying: "Carmen, Carmen, come over here." And your vain side enjoys it. The point is to have the common sense to manage it and not let it dominate you ...

MARISTAIN: *Did Roberto have that common sense?*

PÉREZ DE VEGA: Yes, he did. Listen, sometimes he got overexcited and worked himself up because, as I said before, he had a leader's temperament, a temperament that he never denied. I don't think that Roberto ever deceived anyone. The tales he told in his literary games were something else.

MARISTAIN: *Someone said to me that Bolaño ceased to be a person and became a character ...*

PÉREZ DE VEGA: I think that we have all become characters. When

Roberto died, one of the first things I thought was that part of his work would continue in us, the people who were close to him, and that we'd thus become Roberto's characters. I still think that. Roberto's friend Mihály Dés, the editor of the magazine *Lateral*, which no longer exists, wrote a very good editorial on Roberto's death and said something like that but put it better.[1] When you asked me the other day if Roberto had traveled or not, I said: "Yes, Roberto traveled. The thing is that he magnified everything, because that was how he saw it ..."

MARISTAIN: *What do you mean?*

PÉREZ DE VEGA: Like when he said that he was a great cook. Well, he was a cook whose dishes were sometimes good, sometimes bad, and sometimes ordinary, but he always felt that he was a great cook. His mother was the same. The way he expressed his ideas, as though trying to convince you of something, was exaggerated. He magnified everything. Obviously, he also played a lot of games. Roberto was a very good actor. He'd often convince you of something and then the next day he'd say: "You silly girl, did you really believe that?" He was very playful, very whimsical, someone who enjoyed himself in his work and in his life. Like little children who grow into themselves by playing. He was always very childish, very adolescent, in a good way. He liked to play. His literature had very autobiographical aspects, but it wasn't about recounting reality but making everything he said believable. The best way to believe in something is to make literature out of it. To create a narrative in which it is part of the imaginary universe, the fantasy.

MARISTAIN: *How did you meet?*

PÉREZ DE VEGA: I met him on a train. I was coming back from Zarautz and he got on in Pamplona. I met him through a woman who I went to get a cup of coffee with and with whom I, as Roberto said later, established the kind of intimacy that can arise between women in ten minutes. The woman immediately told me all about her life; I think I said less about mine, because, among other things, it wasn't as interesting as hers. She was a very cultured person and had read a lot. So I stayed in the carriage and she went back to hers, which was two or three cars farther on. I had a headache and she said: "When it passes, come see me." After an hour or two, I can't remember how long, I went to see her, and when I got there she was talking to Roberto. She was a well-read woman who knew about Bolaño. And then she introduced him to me. This was in August 1997. In that carriage, Roberto told me that he was starting to edit *The Savage Detectives*. Then I remember that the woman, Celia, or Cecilia, really a very special person, asked me if I had heard of him and I said that I hadn't. I think that I'm quite well read but I admit that I hadn't read Bolaño. The woman got off in Reus, where she had an apartment and was planning to spend a few days on vacation, and I was left alone with Roberto. I started to think: "What am I going to do with this smarter, more cultured man?" They had been talking about things that I didn't have much to contribute to. I didn't dare get into the conversation, even though I found it so interesting. I remember that when the woman got off the train she asked him from below, "How about Borges?" and Roberto answered, "Borges is God." We went between the carriages so that he could smoke, and I started to feel uncomfortable. I was saying to myself: "This man is too much for me." I felt an urge to leave, but he wouldn't hear of it. That was when he gave me a copy of *Distant Star* and signed it for me. When we arrived, we

had tea in Sants and said goodbye. He took the train to Blanes
and I went home. On the way, I started to read the book. At this
point I should say that there was definitely an attraction. I knew
that I found the man attractive and I found out later that he was
attracted to me, but it was *Distant Star* that really seduced me. I
fell in love with his literary recipe. It was a book that fascinated
me. It was different. I was hungry for a good read, because I'd
been reading bestsellers recommended to me by my friends but
they left me feeling empty. *Distant Star* turned out to be the perfect work by Roberto for me. It's one of the few books that I've
read over and over again.

MARISTAIN: *Had he been promoting his book in Pamplona?*

PÉREZ DE VEGA: He was coming back from a festival organized
by Jesús Ferrero.[2] I think that it was a festival about migration, I
can't remember. Roberto had given a talk there. He was carrying
his red backpack with the Catalan flag, which is common around
here. It was old and beaten up but he kept on using it right to
the end, and he had a few books inside. I suppose he used them
for promotion in Pamplona. I don't know why, but I wrote down
his address while he took my telephone number. I told him that
when I finished the book I would write to him. Three weeks later,
I did. And he, fifteen days after that, called me. At first I didn't
recognize him at all, and he laughed with a laugh as hoarse as his
voice, his broken voice. "You don't know who I am?" he asked.
"It's Roberto." He was answering the letter in which, among
other things, I reminded him of his promise to invite me to dinner when he came to Barcelona. Then he said: "I don't remember
having invited you to dinner." I told him that he had. "Well, well.
We'll have to do that," he said. "I'll send you another book," and
The Skating Rink arrived in the mail. I wrote to him again and he

answered in another letter, and one day in December he called
to tell me that he was coming to Barcelona to have some tests at
the Vall d'Hebron hospital. We went to dinner and took a walk
along El Raval. He showed me his house in Carrer dels Tallers,
and we ended up in the cathedral. The Christmas fair was on in
Santa Lucía, and then I went to pick up my daughter and left him
in Plaza Catalunya so he could take the train back to Blanes. At
the end of the next week he invited me to his house and I went.
We went for breakfast, then to the Botanical Gardens, where
it got late and we were locked in. "We're hungry, what do we
do?" Roberto asked. We started to look around. There were some
buildings behind the gardens and a lady came out of one of them.
We asked her how to get out, and she said that there was a gap
where the fence had broken and told us how to get there. We got
out and went to the port to eat paella.

MARISTAIN: *And so the relationship began . . .*

PÉREZ DE VEGA: Yes. He told me about his family and everything,
and our relationship began.

MARISTAIN: *At the time he was about to publish* The Savage Detectives?

PÉREZ DE VEGA: He was editing *The Savage Detectives* at the time,
and that was very hard on his illness. That really did hurt his liver,
it was really hard work. He saw the galleys after Christmas, and
at the start of '98 he handed the book in to be printed. Then you
know what happened: the Herralde Prize and everything that
went with it. He started to write *Amulet* and got interested in the
dead women of Juárez. One day he asked me, reading an article
about the detention of "the Egyptian": "Do you think he could

be the murderer?" He was very interested in the investigation and followed it closely. He started to write a novel under the title "Corrida," but then gave it up. He was also working on the project *Woes of the True Policeman*, which later made up part of *2666*.

MARISTAIN: *Did his disease cause him physical pain?*

PÉREZ DE VEGA: No, the liver doesn't hurt. But he did get tired easily, more and more at the end. When I met him, he was a slow man, he walked in an almost feline manner, but that wasn't because of the disease. He was like that. What made his life difficult was the tiredness, and editing the huge novels he wrote obviously tired him. "This really gets me down," he used to say.

MARISTAIN: *People always mention his indifference toward his disease. Is that really true?*

PÉREZ DE VEGA: I don't know. When I met him, he took his pills religiously, and took care to eat properly, although he enjoyed his food. One of the things that Roberto enjoyed a lot in his final years was a good meal accompanied by good conversation. We went to buy groceries together, walking to a certain butcher, for example, because it had the cuts that we liked. He asked me to make his favorite dishes, although he was also an austere person who could go whole days with a plate of rice and a bowl of vegetable soup. He was both Spartan and an epicure, the two things at once.

MARISTAIN: *So it all began with* The Savage Detectives*?*

PÉREZ DE VEGA: Hmmm. Actually I think it all began with the publication of *Distant Star*, a book that I think was a watershed because it represents the emergence of a certain kind of literature. That novel is the start of part two, if you will. I think that Roberto was always sure of his worth as a writer.

MARISTAIN: *How did he react to the Herralde Prize?*

PÉREZ DE VEGA: He was very excited. He said to me, "It's one of the few honest prizes left." He was generally a little ambivalent about prizes so it was important to him to point out to me that the Herralde was honest. He was very happy, and the money also was very useful. Roberto knew how to keep fame in its place, which isn't to say that he didn't enjoy it. You write things for publication because you want people to read them. I'm sure that every author who brings out a book would love the opportunity to be number one on the bestseller list even if it was just for a week, and Bolaño was no exception in that regard.

MARISTAIN: *Regarding his disease, is it true that he didn't want to have a transplant?*

PÉREZ DE VEGA: Well, I don't think that he ever said no to the transplant. Carolina would know about that better than I, but I really don't think that he would have refused it. Being in denial about the disease is one thing, but I wouldn't go that far. I don't think that Roberto was in denial about the disease, but about how serious it was. He went for tests every now and again but not as regularly as he needed to, although he took his medication and took care of himself in his own way. However, he tried to avoid the issue and prolonged the decision about the operation for as long as possible. He knew that the only solution was a liver transplant, and his doctor at Vall d'Hebron [Victor García Blasco] told him that regularly. The problem was that if you didn't see it, it became like a superstition, something like "if I can't feel it, it's not there." There are people who don't go to the doctor because they think that if they go the doctor will find something. I think like that. I hate going to the doctor, so from that standpoint I understood Roberto, but I also told him that he had to do the tests again, that time was passing and his disease was extremely silent … Eventually the day came when he finally put himself on the list for the transplant. He'd been waiting a year and half for the operation when he died.

MARISTAIN: *Did his mother tell him to take care of himself?*

PÉREZ DE VEGA: His mother was very worried and fretful. The thing was that you couldn't tell Roberto to do things. Insisting on things he didn't want to talk about meant having to accept the distance that came afterward. He wasn't stupid. Signing up for a transplant is, I think, a tough, difficult, and very personal decision. A lot of things go through your head. You need someone to die so that you can live, you think that maybe you've already done everything you were supposed to do and now it's all over for you. I don't know, everyone has their own process. Roberto really didn't like putting himself in the doctors' hands, manipulating his body, making decisions about him. I think that it was also a question of embarrassment, he was horrified by all that. Finally he took the bull by the horns, accepted the seriousness of the illness and put himself on the list. Waiting for a transplant is very tough, you start in thirtieth place and count down from there. When Easter came, I think he was fourth and Roberto said: "They'll call me now, a lot of accidents happen during Easter week." He was second in line when he died.

MARISTAIN: *What were his final days like?*

PÉREZ DE VEGA: He got back from Seville on June 28. I went to pick him up at the airport. On Sunday afternoon I went to Barcelona to pick up my daughter, who was with her father. On Monday, June 30, he called to ask me to pick him up because he felt bad; he'd coughed up blood. He had had a similar episode two months before and hadn't wanted to do anything about it because it went away. Something we all do. I went to pick him up immediately because he had varicose veins in his esophagus and I knew that that could be fatal. Roberto had a persistent cough, he was a little congested, and it was very hot, which wasn't good for his varicose veins because, as you know, high temperatures cause dilation and swelling throughout the body … So I went to Blanes to pick him up, he'd been doing some paperwork with Carolina and that day had finished *The Insufferable Gaucho* and wanted to take it to the publisher. I said to him: "We can print it out in Barcelona, we're leaving now." All I wanted to do was take him to the hospital. But he said that he was fine. His face was pale but he'd barely slept. The day before, he had been with his son, made him some macaroni and then took him back to his mother's house that morning because he knew that he had to go to Barcelona. Roberto wanted to take *The Insufferable Gaucho* to the publishers before going to the hospital. When I got there and saw how ill he looked, I knew that that wasn't a good idea but there was nothing I could do. So we went to Barcelona, I went to buy some things, then we got home, printed out *The Insufferable Gaucho*, and when I tried to give him the disk he told me to keep it. That was how I ended up with the disk. Then we went to the publisher. I left him there for about two hours, and when I came to pick him up he didn't want to go to the hospital anymore. I thought for a moment about making him get out of the car and driving off because the situation made me very angry, but I knew that that wasn't the solution. So we went to Blanes. We stopped in one of the service areas that we both loved. We ate some tortilla and set out for his house, where I left him. I had to get back to Barcelona to get my daughter, although I wasn't thinking completely clearly at the time. I was very worried, so I called a friend to ask her to take care of my daughter. While I was doing that, Roberto came out onto the balcony to say, "Carmen, when you get back, call me because I don't have any credit." I said to myself: "I'm not leaving him like this without a phone." I went up. It was eleven at night and we were both very tired.

At two thirty in the morning, he woke me up to tell me that he needed something to eat. It was true, he hadn't eaten anything since that afternoon, which could give him hypoglycemia. I insisted that he go to the hospital because I suspected that he was swallowing blood, but he started to cook some rice. On the first bite, he vomited a horrendous amount of blood, and of course that was when he decided to go to the hospital. He had time to put on some music, the song "Lucha de gigantes."[3] He had time to have a shower, and I think that he thought that all that would keep the disease at bay, although in fact it was doing just the opposite. "Lucha de gigantes," which he often played, was the last song he ever heard. While he was taking his shower I gathered some things, I told him to hurry up ...

At one point I thought about calling an ambulance, but knowing Roberto I realized that that was a bad idea so I took him in the car. I remember the empty highway and my little car battling as best it could against a strong wind blowing in the other direction. Finally we got to the hospital at about four thirty in the morning. We parked, went up the ramp to the Emergency Room, and I looked at him: he was calm, dignified, and elegant. Suddenly he took me by the hand and asked: "How are you?"

While we waited for the doctors I ended up sitting on a bed and he sat on a chair telling those bad jokes he used to tell. He told the famous bad joke he had told in Seville.[4] I think that it was his way of distancing himself from what was happening. I was obviously hysterical, although I was trying not to show it. We spent several hours in the Emergency Room. I spent the night with him, and the next day he was transferred to the Bleeds Unit, where there weren't any beds. He didn't want to go there. He was fine in the Emergency Room, where a doctor whose name I don't remember—I don't know if I'd recognize her now—treated us wonderfully. She took care of both him and me. (His doctor, Víctor Vargas, was out of the city.) That night, Roberto asked her: "Doctor, I'm not coming out of this hospital, am I?" And the doctor said: "No, no, of course you'll get out, Roberto, you'll leave this hospital." Roberto really didn't want to be in the Bleeds Unit because, among other things, he couldn't have people with him there. While we were in the Emergency Room, I could spend the whole night with him, then Carolina came to relieve me and she was able to stay too. He was very sick, but right up until the final moments, he was still embarrassed. He didn't want the nurse to touch him, he didn't let strangers get too close to him. When he got trapped with all those tubes and catheters, that's when I think he definitively went downhill. The last time I saw him was when they took him to the Bleeds Unit. He gave me his glasses, and now, looking back, I think that that was when he resigned himself to death. Only then, and not before, as lots of people have tried to say, did he see death at his side. Roberto had always chosen life. He knew that he might die, of course, but he also knew that he might live. He had children, he had a responsibility toward them. They were the most important thing in the world to him. Also, it's not true that in anticipating his death he set himself to write *2666* as economic support for his children. He was always going to write that novel, whatever happened.

MARISTAIN: *In fact, 2666 wasn't the last thing he wrote . . .*

PÉREZ DE VEGA: That's what I was saying. With Roberto it is very difficult to separate his personal and professional lives. He was, as Bruno Montané says, "a man-work." The unfinished part of *2666* is the part with the crimes. He wrote the Archimboldi section first. The last words written for that novel were written in February 2003. The rest of the time he spent living and doing other things. The crimes, one after another, were too much for him. It was very hard work. He said that he couldn't cope with any more crimes. He wanted to save his energy to recover from the transplant. That was when he started to put together *The Insufferable Gaucho*. He wrote two new stories, "The Insufferable Gaucho" and "Police Rat." He put together that book because he said that it would be his economic support for the postoperative period. He said: "This will give me the freedom to finish *2666* and edit it." Also, he wasn't writing so intensely anymore. Two whole days could go by without him turning on the computer. What people say about him writing right up until the night before his death is a very nice, literary story, but it's not true.

MARISTAIN: *When Roberto died and you took a backseat, do you think that's what he would have expected of you?*

PÉREZ DE VEGA: Right now, I'm not thinking about what he would have expected of me. I'm doing what I think I need to do. Roberto's memory is of course reflected in my actions, and the most important thing to him was his children. He had young children, one of them a very young daughter, and they needed to be cared for. It wasn't right to cause a fuss and tarnish his memory. All Roberto and I promised each other was friendship and respect. That is what I wanted and want to preserve. I considered myself his woman, and he once told me that I would be his last love. Well, there it is, it was very nice and fine, but no one could have anticipated how big his posthumous figure would become. I think that Roberto's posthumous fame is an autonomous, greedy entity that threatens to swallow up everything. Roberto left things as well organized as he could and wanted to at that time, because, among other things, we all thought that the transplant would be a success and that he was going to live.

MARISTAIN: *I understand what you say about friendship and respect, but I also understand the anger at things people have said—an anger you never express, in any case ...*

PÉREZ DE VEGA: Well, there are many phases to grief. When a loved one dies, there's denial, a lot of anger, and a mixture of all kinds of things. There's also the guilt stage. I feel guilty for a lot of things. The moment at the hospital ... It's easy to say things in retrospect, but in such an extreme situation, such a difficult one for me and everyone who loved Roberto, a moment comes when things get out of hand. You can't control things anymore. His mother, sister, Carolina, Bruno [Montané] were all at the hospital ...

MARISTAIN: *Who was the first person you turned to when Roberto died?*

PÉREZ DE VEGA: A friend. María Salomé came out and said: "Carmen, it's over ..." I ran out of the hospital, crying disconsolately, and then my tears all dried up. It was very difficult to start crying again. I got back to reality on the afternoon after his death. It was July 15 and I was at a friend's house. When I left I went back the way I always went with Roberto, and then I was suddenly aware of the emptiness and horror that awaited me. The tears started to flow on the train, and I said to myself: "Roberto has died."

16

The Siren Songs Are Deafening

With certain precautions—The shitstorms—Pessoa's trunk

Jorge Herralde remembers Roberto Bolaño as one of the writers he was closest to. He spent many hours chatting about literature, and it counted for a lot that Roberto loved the list put out by Anagrama, the publisher Herralde founded in 1969.

"It had all the writers he liked, from Nabokov to Perec, Piglia to Pitol, and many others. Over the eight years of our personal and professional relationship, we published nine or ten of his books. The first, *Distant Star*, is a treasure. His reputation was made with *The Savage Detectives*. Young Latin American writers started to love him, but the seniors regarded him with caution.

"Then came the great posthumous triumph of *2666*, which is one of the most unusual and interesting phenomena to have occurred in good Spanish literature in the last fifty years," Herralde says. "With *The Savage Detectives* he went up a notch and even started to be well regarded by American critics who are usually hostile to translations."

MARISTAIN: *If you had to, how would you compare the Bolaño boom to the Latin American boom?*

HERRALDE: Well, the thing about the boom is, as is well known, that it happened to a set of excellent writers. In contrast, Bolaño is a more isolated case: he's like a sniper shooting from Blanes, a small town near Barcelona, and without any desire to triumph in a material sense. Living just for literature, he nonetheless achieves this unprecedented success.

MARISTAIN: *He would have liked that you called him a sniper . . .*

HERRALDE: Ha-ha. Yes, of course. That's how he felt.

MARISTAIN: *Was he a cultured man?*

HERRALDE: Cultured, no. He was extremely cultured. He had an excellent knowledge of French literature, especially poetry, which can clearly be seen in *The Savage Detectives*. He read his contemporaries, which isn't that common among writers, and read them passionately, whether he approved of their work or not. Another unusual thing was that he didn't speak much about his own work but did talk about other writers and hundreds of other subjects that interested him.

MARISTAIN: *He didn't speak about what he wrote. He wrote.*

HERRALDE: He wrote, read, and watched television. That was essentially all he did.

MARISTAIN: *As an editor, could you discuss the state of his books before they were published?*

HERRALDE: Yes, but I have to say that he presented his books when they were at a stage of readiness, which was unusual. They were on a computer, with wide, long columns, almost without any typos: very clean and at the same time very well thought out and finished. As you know, there was a small disagreement about the title of *By Night in Chile*: he wanted to call it *Tormenta de mierda* (Shitstorm) . . . I, not exactly the most prudish of people, thought that we might discourage a certain kind of buyer, the more prudish kind, with that title. So I said to him: "Listen, I think that

By Night in Chile is much better." At the same time, without my knowing it, Juan Villoro was flatly against "*Shitstorm*," and between us we were able to convince him. It wasn't easy because he was pretty tenacious and stuck by his convictions. He thought that right from the start it gave Pinochet the punch he wanted to give him with that book.

With *The Savage Detectives*, throughout the middle part in which there are innumerable vignettes and short stories, I thought that a bit of cutting would do some good. We argued about it and finally came to a compromise. He agreed to cut two of the sections and then refused to discuss the other two. I said that it was his book and that the tiny difference was nothing. "In any case, your novel is a masterwork," I told him.

MARISTAIN: *Would you say that you were perfect for each other?*

HERRALDE: I don't know that I'd go so far, but there was a general harmony between us. We also had his translation rights and acted as his agents, and I was very pleased with that. We were lucky enough to get him published in Germany, France, Italy ...

MARISTAIN: *What is your opinion of the publication of his books after his death?*

HERRALDE: I'd say it was a little strange. According to Ignacio Echevarría, who was studying all the material left behind by Roberto, there were only a few stories, outlines or stubs of novels, poems and miscellany—in other words, nothing important. So he just took charge of the last story collection, and then *The Unknown University* came out, which was sort of the blueprint for the poetry that came out later. When his literary agent made that surprise announcement about a new novel called *The Third Reich*, the negotiations began. They were long, complex, and delicate, but we finally reached an agreement to buy *The Third Reich*, which I think is a good first novel. It's not perfect but it has certainly got admirable qualities. If it had been sent to me to read I would have published it. A few days ago I got an e-mail from the agent saying that another novel has surfaced [*Woes of the True Policeman*], which he'll give me to read at the Frankfurt Book Fair. Supposedly it contains the origins for *2666* and *The Savage Detectives*. But this is beginning to be a little like Pessoa's trunk, a bottomless trunk ... I don't know.

MARISTAIN: *Do you ever speak to Carolina?*

HERRALDE: No, I haven't spoken to her in a while.

MARISTAIN: *Why do you think Roberto never went back to Mexico?*

HERRALDE: He didn't feel like it, he didn't want to ... I don't know whether he had very good memories. Also, all that happened long ago, that experience of exile, although he wasn't exiled in the classic sense. He didn't have a good relationship with his father. They met in Madrid one day, his father was visiting with his new wife, and it so happened that I was at the Wellington Hotel too, and I recommended it to them because we always go there. At about nine, my wife, Laly, Álvaro Pombo, and I came back for dinner and Roberto was there with Carolina, a little shattered by the day he had spent with his father.

MARISTAIN: *Was he very close to his mother?*

HERRALDE: Yes, he loved her very much. His mother was the first to go to Catalonia. They were always together.

MARISTAIN: *Who would you say was really close to Roberto in the last few years?*

HERRALDE: During his final years, his mother above all. There was a sister who also lived in Figueras, I think, who he didn't see so much. There wasn't so much feeling between them, although they got on well. And then there were his friends from Barcelona—I'd say especially Ignacio Echevarría, Rodrigo Fresán, Antonio Porta, and us.

MARISTAIN: *Was he a difficult man?*

HERRALDE: No, no, not at all. It was in Chile where he ... let's say he wasn't particularly nice, to put it mildly, especially not to sacred cows like Isabel Allende, Skármeta, et al. But most of the major groups of fairly good writers don't compare to Bolaño. Isabel Allende got very annoyed and said that Roberto was a very unpleasant person, that he didn't like anyone, which isn't true. The thing was that he was against certain writers with whom he had nothing in common, he didn't like their literature or how they had used their talent. Bolaño was generous, I'd say excessively generous with young writers.

MARISTAIN: *Which book did you enjoy the most?*

HERRALDE: It's difficult to choose. His two big novels, *2666* and *The Savage Detectives*, are masterpieces, very ambitious and very well done, but he also has jewels like *Distant Star* and *By Night in Chile*. Stories like "Sensini," based on the Argentinian writer Antonio de Benedetto, which is about literary competitions, which were very important to Roberto. These books didn't get him much money but helped him through his most penurious moments.

MARISTAIN: *Did it hurt you that Carolina López took the rights to his books away from you?*

HERRALDE: A lot. Especially because it was clearly undeserved. I never had a disagreement with Bolaño, I never had a disagreement with Carolina López. The truth is that I don't know what happened. Either wires got crossed or the relationship was soured by other people. She unilaterally decided to break with Ignacio Echevarría, the man who took charge of Roberto's work, with me, and with Anagrama. This job is wonderful, though it's not easy, can be difficult, but by its nature it offers great joy and huge disappointments. It's a roller coaster. As I said in an article once, it's about doling out and receiving pain. Doling out pain to so many manuscripts that one has to reject. If it's an author you have no ties to, they experience the pain. When it's an author who has published several books with you but you decide not to continue with, it's painful for the publisher as well as for the author. And then there is the pain when there are misunderstandings with authors who are very much to the publisher's liking but who decide to listen to siren songs, which can be deafening.

The Little Bolaños

Reading desperately—Builder, gardener, taxi driver—The older brother—He read the same kind of things as we did—From Neostalinists to Opus Dei—The twenty-first century began in 1998—He didn't adapt, he didn't sell out. He didn't want to fit in—The Chilean pioneer—The little Bolaños—The Virgin of Tepeyac looked at me, winked, and blessed me—Next to a school, on the shore of the river—An empty street—A man with a dog on the beach—In comparison to him I'd read nothing—The romantic advisor—The love isn't there—He always ate my dessert if it was chocolate

Adolfo Bioy Casares used to say that a good writer inspires his readers to write.

Since Roberto Bolaño's death in 2003, new generations of authors have echoed his voice, expanding the Chilean writer's legacy almost infinitely.

Bolaño would surely give all of them the advice of Bioy Casares: "I take the liberty of advising people to write, because it is like adding a room to the house of life. It is life and it is thinking about life, which is another way to experience it more intensely."

In Mexico, where Bolaño is considered a Mexican author, a new crop of novels appeared in the years after his death, books that owed a big debt to his work and seemed to follow in the same tradition. Take Juan Pablo Villalobos, the author of *Fiesta en la madriguera* (Party in the Early Hours). Critics instantly noted the connection to Bolaño's fiction, with one critic saying that the book had "burst forth from the crimes section of *2666*."

About the resemblance, Villalobos says, "Roberto Bolaño is undoubtedly a very strong reference for everyone currently writing today."[1] He has also written about his introduction to Bolaño:

I read *The Savage Detectives* in three days. During those days I did only three things: I ate pizza (while reading), went to the bathroom (still reading), and slept (dreaming about what I'd read). I was going through a terrible moment in my life, and all I wanted to do was read Bolaño. I read desperately. I read as though the answer to my troubles lay in those 622 pages. As if reading the book without stopping was a magic spell, an occult formula, or a prayer. And it worked. When I finished I was even more depressed and angry, but I had renewed faith in literature and it strengthened my vocation as a writer.[2]

To the Mexican writer Edson Lechuga, Roberto Bolaño was the last true writer to dedicate his life to writing.[3] A man who threw himself off the sixth floor of a building with his eyes wide open just to see what would happen as he fell. To him, Roberto Bolaño is a writer on the same level as Gabriel García Márquez and Juan Rulfo.

"He had an influence on me and I hope a lot of others, a whole generation. Julián Herbert, Juan Pablo Villalobos, Valeria Luiselli ... In my case it was clear," he admits.

The entire Bolaño universe is aimed at creating a new canon and includes writers as diverse as the members of the Hora Zero group in Peru, which was linked directly to the Infrarealists, and new voices in Chilean literature.

Rodrigo Díaz Cortez, born in Santiago de Chile in 1977, is one of these voices. With his incipient but unique style, he is sure to attract a lot of attention from readers and critics in the future. He won the twelfth Mario Vargas Llosa Prize for the novel with *Tridente del plata* (Silver Trident), a story set in the 1980s and '90s in Santiago de Chile and Valparaíso, and used the prize money to buy a taxi driver's license to work in Barcelona. His book *Poeta bajo el mar* (Poet Under the Sea) was a finalist in the *Qué Leer* and the City of Barbastro Prizes.

Díaz Cortez, who has lived in Barcelona for more than a decade, is often described as having followed in Roberto Bolaño's footsteps in Spain, especially because of the many different jobs he has had to support himself. First, he took care of a quadriplegic aunt, then he was a gardener, a builder, and worked in a factory assembling metallic structures. Currently, in addition to driving his taxi, he gives fiction classes at the Aula de Escritores, a literary and film school in the center of Grácia. He has recently published the novel *El peor de los guerreros* (The Worst Warrior).

MARISTAIN: *Is new Chilean fiction contaminated by Roberto Bolaño?*

DÍAZ CORTEZ: I suppose so. Recently I've been disconnected from Chile. I hear from other writers that the majority write like Alberto Fuguet, while the others write like Bolaño: polar opposites. In any case, I couldn't answer you for sure because not many books from Chile get to Spain.

MARISTAIN: *Do you think that Roberto Bolaño is more a poet than a prose writer, or is it the other way around?*

DÍAZ CORTEZ: The two things go hand in hand. I think that he was a prose writer–poet and a poet–prose writer. The first book I read by Roberto was *Distant Star*, a book that I found in Chile when I was very young. Then I read the stories, which I very much enjoyed. What most interests me about him is that I see him as part of a generation that had almost been orphaned, that had no support from established writers. Taking literature to unprecedented limits, which is what he did with *The Savage Detectives* and *2666*, was another of his talents.

MARISTAIN: *Why did you decide to go to the street-naming ceremony in his honor?*

DÍAZ CORTEZ: It was important to me to be there, to accompany my poet friends, including Jorge Morales, who's a real all-terrain vehicle. Then there's all the symbolism: what it means to have a street named after you, a space, a place, as Jorge said, to go to cut back the weeds. I think that we all came here to in some way share this moment with Roberto, even if it's only in our imaginations. Roberto is a kind of older-brother figure to young Chilean writers.

• • •

Of all the young voices in Chilean literature, the one that comes up most often in relation to Bolaño is the respected writer and poet Alejandro Zambra, who was born in Santiago de Chile in 1975. His books *Bonsai* (for which he won the Chilean Critics' Prize), *The Private Lives of Trees*, and *Ways of Going Home* (winner of the Altazor Prize) were all published by Anagrama. He has already taken part in several conferences dedicated to Bolaño, including the 2010 homage organized by the Casa de América in Madrid, for which Ignacio Echevarría acted as advisor.

Zambra says that "many readers feel close to Bolaño, because when he appeared he was clearly reading similar things to what we were reading. Especially with regard to Chilean literature: Nicanor Parra and Enrique Lihn, two poets whom Bolaño read a lot. I see him as a kind of big brother, who tells you all about his adventures."

When asked whether Roberto is more of a poet or a prose writer, Zambra immediately calls the division "artificial."

They are different facets of the same literature. Bolaño's poetry is in one sense what Roberto Bolaño's characters write, and vice versa. The novels are written with a gaze that both narrates and disassociates itself from the traditional mechanisms of fiction.

So I think it's difficult to read his poetry separately from his fiction; at the same time, his fiction depends upon his poetry.

Bolaño's death gave rise to retrospective declarations of friendship and hidden skirmishes that could very well be described as Bolaño-esque. Later, the posthumous publication of *2666* generated debates that had very little to do with the novel. The funniest moment in the discourse was the incredible answer of a wounded writer: He brazenly told *El Mercurio* that he hadn't read the novel but that didn't mean that he couldn't offer his opinion of it. Chilean literature sees itself as a proudly separate island that welcomes tourists with open arms, but regards its prodigal sons with suspicion … He was, of course, the greatest Hispano-American writer of his generation, and beyond the literary disputes, the fact is that we will be reading and rereading him for several decades with the same excitement.

Zambra continues:

So, is Bolaño the new Parra or José Donoso of Chilean literature? It's an absurd question, but in a notable article on Donoso, Bolaño answered it: "Neostalinists and Opus Dei, thugs on the right and the left, feminists and the poor machos of Santiago, all of them, overtly or not, claim to be disciples of Donoso. That's a serious mistake. They'd do better to read him. They'd do better to stop writing and read him. It's much better to read." In any case—and this is where Borges comes in, although he was never really away—Bolaño doesn't have successors, only precursors: voices we haven't yet discovered but that undoubtedly lurk in the pages of *Amulet*, *By Night in Chile*, and *2666*. Chilean readers of Bolaño are also readers of Wilcock, Enrique Vila-Matas and Sergio Pitol, Ricardo Piglia and Rodrigo Fresán, Fernando

Vallejo, Enrique Lihn, and other authors who don't necessarily appear on must-read lists.[4]

• • •

Rodrigo Fresán says that many people would pay a lot of money for the house at number 2666 on the new Carrer de Roberto Bolaño in Gerona. For now, it is a sunny street on the outskirts of the city, surrounded by a *rambla* with a stone plaza in the Domeny neighborhood.

The man behind the renaming initiative was the Chilean poet and writer Jorge Morales, the cofounder, along with Albert Compte (who died in 2011 at the age of forty-seven), of the literary project *El Llop Ferotge*. He admits that Roberto Bolaño is a "passion" of his.

"I first read him in 2002," says Morales. "Milan Kundera once remarked on the incredible way in which one can discover authors in the world of literature through books that one realizes later on perhaps weren't that important but that serve to set up a more meaningful revelation. I had that kind of revelation with Bolaño ... When I started to read the story 'Sensini' [collected in *Last Evenings on Earth*]. I was very poor in Gerona," he continues. "I was an illegal immigrant, like Bolaño when he lived here. I had got to Gerona in 2001, seeking a path that was related to poetry. Reading Bolaño helped me to see that anything is possible."

Of course, to Morales, a ravenous wolf with an excellent nose for good-quality literature, the work of the writer for whom he would one day organize a naming ceremony was far from incidental.

"The twenty-first century began in 1998 with the publication of *The Savage Detectives*. And I think that says it all," concludes Morales.

MARISTAIN: *You were twenty-six when you experienced this revelation ... Is it possible to say that Bolaño's literature should be classified in the category of literature to be read when one is young?*

MORALES: I don't think so. *2666*, for example, could easily be considered a great book of contemporary history. The best study of the twentieth century I've ever read is contained in that novel. It's true that younger generations were the first to welcome Bolaño's book with enthusiasm and euphoria. And I think that that's because he never grew old. He didn't adapt, he didn't sell out. He didn't want to fit in, but held on to the same rebellious spirit to the end. That same spirit led him to found the Infrarealist movement in 1976, and to go back to Chile to fight for the revolution and for socialism in 1973.

MARISTAIN: *He said that if he hadn't been a writer he'd have been a detective, but I think that he would have been a rock star ...*

MORALES: The thing is that you have to be able to sing. All writers and detectives have sung under their breath in the shower, but ...

MARISTAIN: *What one might call "Chilean-ness" is very diluted in Roberto's work. As a Chilean writer, do you see it like that?*

MORALES: Look, I recently read an interview with a young Chilean author in *El País*, and he said that Roberto wasn't a Chilean author but a Mexican or Catalan one. I've lived in Gerona for ten years, and I can tell you that for progressive, cultured Catalans it would be a source of pride for Bolaño to be described as a Catalan writer, but to the average Catalan who doesn't read much, Bolaño is just another South American, clearly a Latin

American author. He answered the question himself: "I'm Latin American." Declaring that one is Latin American isn't an innocent affirmation. The concept of being Latin American was conceived of by a great thinker, the Chilean Francisco Bilbao. He saw our continent as a unit, a whole and a process. The inhabitants of Latin America have a shared identity and, especially, shared problems. In Bolaño's case, there are many Chilean things in his literature. The city of Los Ángeles, Chile, for example, which I went to one summer as a child, or the recent political history of our country. Also, Bolaño's political assessment of recent Chilean history is unique. He avoids the dogmas of the left and right and appeals to more universal values.

MARISTAIN: *There is still a lot of resistance coming from within Chilean literature. Many people still refuse to accept Roberto Bolaño...*

MORALES: To start with, Chile doesn't belong to the Chileans, just as Mexico doesn't belong to the Mexicans. In Chile, the right boasted for a long time about being the most English country in Latin America. Why should I care about the canon in my country when I've discovered Alejandro Zambra, an author from my generation who has written three novels bursting with life in the new style, here, in the bookstore Librería 22 in Gerona? I looked on the Internet to see what people were saying about Zambra in Chile, and it was just rubbish. They said, for example, that there were other Chileans who deserved to be in the Anagrama catalog more than Zambra ... You can imagine that while Chilean literary criticism is still mediocre and ordinary, I really don't care whether they accept Roberto Bolaño or not. I'm much more interested in seeing how the rest of the world values literary work that will certainly transcend us.

MARISTAIN: *Who else would you mention as being part of the new Chilean literature?*

MORALES: Kato Ramone, Álvaro Bisama, Rodrigo Díaz Cortez ... "The Little Bolaños," as we're called in Chile.[5] There is a common, incorruptible critical spirit, and also an escape from Spanish influences, making more use of humor and irony.

MARISTAIN: *How does one escape the Bolaño myth? How does one deconstruct the media and marketing myth that shrouds his posthumous figure?*

MORALES: I think that that's a problem for new readers of Roberto Bolaño. For those who haven't read him yet. I'm not interested in the myth. When I start to read articles of doubtful provenance that focus on his private life or his presumed, nonexistent addiction to heroin, something that played well in the American market so that Bolaño would fit in with the beatniks, I throw it away immediately. For example, the fact that Gerona, a city with seven hundred thousand inhabitants, has a street named after a Latin American is news, but an article has just come out in *La Tercera* speculating on whether his widow or last partner would come, and that seems horrible to me. That's not cultural journalism at all. I expect that of *Hello* magazine, not a cultural supplement.

MARISTAIN: *What was the Bolaño of Gerona like?*

MORALES: He was a twenty-eight-year-old man who already had a past in literature. He had founded the Infrarealist movement, et cetera. His arrival in the city must have been tough. Gerona has changed a lot in the last few years. Bolaño got here by chance. Just because his sister was here. María Salomé [Bolaño] was married to a Catalan, Narcís Batallé, and they'd decided to go to Mexico and leave the place they had in Gerona. It's not somewhere he chose to live. Today, you can start literary and cultural projects in Gerona, but that wasn't the case twenty-five years ago. When Bolaño got here, all the action in the city was focused on a single street. It was the kind of place where people left for work early and got home late. Roberto spent the autumn in a place where he didn't have to pay rent, and he spent the summer working in the Estrella de Mar campsite …

MARISTAIN: *Was his time in Gerona the period when he was poorest?*

MORALES: Well, I don't know how poor he had been in Barcelona. People from the time tell me that Bolaño was poor, but then everyone was poor. There wasn't even a public library as there is now, where you can go to read, pass the time in the warmth, surrounded by books.

MARISTAIN: *So when you got to Gerona you started to hear stories about Roberto …*

MORALES: It was great, reading the stories and then being in some of the places where they are set. Then I started to get to know characters like Ponç Puigdevall, and Guillem Terribas at Librería 22, and it was very easy to put together Roberto Bolaño's time in the city. This was where he wrote "Autumn Prose in Gerona" and the notes for *Advice from a Disciple of Morrison to a Fan of Joyce*, the novel he cowrote with A. G. Porta that was published in 1983.[6]

• • •

"One day Calle Bucareli will be called Calle Roberto Bolaño": it was easy to think like that. It was very seductive and magical to imagine oneself walking in the area near La Habana Café, close to the corner of the offices of *La Prensa* in Mexico City where journalists of different and often contrasting kinds gather in fraternal camaraderie; *El Universal* was on Bucareli; around the corner, on Reforma, was *La Prensa* and *Excélsior*; a few blocks away, on Morelos, was *Milenio*.

Neither is it ridiculous to imagine that in Colonia Guadalupe Tepeyac, where Bolaño grew into a man watching millions— yes, millions—of pilgrims pass by on their way to the Basilica of Guadalupe, where rest the remains of Juan Diego, the Native American to whom, according to Catholic belief, the Virgin Mary appeared in 1531, Calle Samuel might one day bear the name of the author of *The Savage Detectives*.

The house of the Bolaño-Ávalos family sat a little over ten blocks from the Basilica, a short distance away from the flow of tourists who flock to one of the must-see sights of Mexico City. Bolaño went there once to accompany the Chilean poet Jaime Quezada, who wanted to buy some holy souvenirs to send to his mother in Santiago: "I have my photo taken on a little cardboard and stone horse. Bolaño handsomely follows my example. 'A souvenir,' he says ... Coming out of the Basilica I buy votive offerings with images of the Virgin, colored postcards ... And Roberto, standing next to me, says: 'The Virgin of Tepeyac looked at me, winked, and blessed me. And I bowed to her.' "[7]

Yet it is in Gerona, where he arrived in 1980 at age twenty-eight and lived "very badly," according to Guillem Terribas, for six years, that Roberto Bolaño has a street named after him.

In Gerona he met his wife. It was in Gerona, according to a letter he sent to his sister, María Salomé, that Roberto thought he might have found somewhere where he could be happy.

Jorge Morales says, "Next to a school, on the shore of the river, where they've built sports fields now, and a lot of gardens and trees, all very green, there will be a place where we can go to enjoy the summer, smoke a cigarette, and read his poems."

MARISTAIN: *Tell me the story of Carrer de Roberto Bolaño.*

MORALES: The story goes back to 2008, when we were about to publish the project *El Llop Ferotge*. The eighth edition of the magazine would be entirely dedicated to Roberto Bolaño, to analyzing his work. There were texts by Alejandro Zambra, Álvaro Bisama, and Ponç Puigdevall, and we also published snippets from a magazine he published with his friend Bruno Montané, which was called *Berthe Trépat*, in homage to one of the characters in *Hopscotch* by Julio Cortázar. We launched that edition of *El Llop Ferotge* in front of a large crowd and presented a formal petition to the council asking for the city to name a street after Roberto Bolaño. In December 2009, the municipal council of Gerona, by unanimous consensus of all parties, decided to name a street after him, to be opened on June 18, 2011.

MARISTAIN: *How did you find out about the municipality's decision?*

MORALES: I was in Chile. I had been in Patagonia for a while and went somewhere where they had Internet. When I got online, I saw an e-mail from the council informing me of the decision. I was with my partner and there were a couple of Chileans with us, the kind who work with animals and have no idea who Bolaño is.

Many of the stories he tells happen in the street, not to mention his legendary walks with his friend Mario Santiago Papasquiaro. José Martí says that the role of a poet consists of singing the praises of all that is beautiful, sparking enthusiasm for all that is noble, and admiring everything great. The beautiful, the noble, and the great are the materials we work with. One reads a lot of books, and many of them are very good, but to have found someone capable of taking literature to such great heights is cause for celebration. During the naming ceremony for Carrer de Roberto Bolaño, Ignacio Echevarría invited those present to "laugh hard at all this, as he would have done," especially when he found out that the street to be named in his honor would be an empty one.

I guess that Roberto Bolaño, who wrote so much about forgotten writers, would like the kind of oblivion that comes with having a street in your name. He'd like that, in a hundred or two hundred years, in one of those fantasies about the future that he enjoyed so much, it would be full of cinemas, bars, and children and adults saying their address, "Roberto Bolaño 25, second floor," without knowing who on earth Roberto Bolaño was, which is what happens with street names.

• • •

Ponç Puigdevall looks as though he's stepped straight out of a novel by Roberto Bolaño. Not melancholy or defeated, he is just as solitary as when he first wandered the streets of Gerona, when his only company was his dog Gaita. The Catalan author of *Un silenci sec* (A Dry Silence), *Era un secret* (It Was a Secret), *Àlbum Galmés* (The Galmés Album), and *Un dia tranquil* (A Quiet Day) walks down the rambla of San Feliu de Guíxols with a German shepherd who, like its master, has a bark that's worse than its bite.

It's understandable that Bolaño felt drawn to a man like Ponç from the first, with his catastrophically bleak view of the world and its inhabitants, protected by a hard shell that only makes his charming vulnerability all the more obvious.

MARISTAIN: *What was the first book you read by Roberto Bolaño?*

PUIGDEVALL: *Nazi Literature in the Americas.* At the time I was a literary critic and I'd never heard of him. I didn't know who he was, but both the title and the cover caught my eye. I read it, liked it a lot, and immediately afterward *Distant Star* was published, which was something new to me. It was South American literature of a kind we'd never seen from there before. All of us who read and write about literature in some ways educated ourselves directly from the boom, the novels of Gabriel García Márquez and Mario Vargas Llosa. In contrast, Bolaño's work belonged to another generation and was thus much closer to our interests and aesthetic. He was a new discovery, an author who is much closer to younger people.

MARISTAIN: *What was it that most attracted your attention about how he wrote?*

PUIGDEVALL: First, the courage. A book like *Nazi Literature in the Americas,* with no compunction or false modesty, is another *Universal History of Infamy.* Here, you can see all the hallmarks of the literature of Roberto Bolaño, the moral and aesthetic courage to place himself on the same level as Borges. He is a pretty daring writer. There's also another of his preoccupations: literature itself. *Nazi Literature in the Americas* is a dictionary of fictitious authors. Then there's that instinct for the new, the air of unknown that you can sense in the complexly simple writing.

MARISTAIN: *The constant flight from cliché and florid writing deriving from his harsh sense of humor…*

PUIGDEVALL: Yes, that's true too. It's an ironic humor that could be very savage when he wanted it to be.

MARISTAIN: *How did you meet him?*

PUIGDEVALL: Well, at the time I had the misfortune to live in Gerona. I went to the Librería 22 bookstore where there was a bookseller called Felip Ortega,[8] who later went on to manage the Casa del Libro in Barcelona and then set up another bookshop. He was an unusual bookseller because he read the books that he sold, and we would always chat about his new discoveries. When Bolaño published *Phone Calls*, I told him to read it and he was immediately interested in holding an event at the store. They got in contact, and Ortega asked me to introduce the book. That night was an important moment for literature because it saw the meeting of Javier Cercas and Roberto Bolaño.[9] Later, when I published my book *Era un secret* (It Was a Secret), I asked Bolaño to introduce it at the launch, and there I met the person who would become his poetry editor, Jaume Vallcorba.[10] After that, Bolaño and I became friends. We saw each other occasionally. He didn't drive and neither did I, but we spoke on the telephone a lot. Also he had the poor taste to live in Blanes, which was quite difficult to get to because of the buses and trains, but we managed to see each other.

MARISTAIN: *How would you portray him?*

PUIGDEVALL: I'd start with how I noticed that he didn't drink. The second thing would be that he smoked a lot, more than me. The third is that I thought I had read everything, but in comparison to him I'd read nothing. I also thought that I'd seen every film and could remember all of them, but no, I was wrong. He also gave a lot of advice, about life and everyday things, and I regret not listening to him, because I always did the wrong thing. Bolaño also had a sense of humor that could be a great consolation to those who are habitually depressed and in a bad mood.

MARISTAIN: *He was a little insistent with his advice...*

PUIGDEVALL: Yes. The natural reaction was not to listen to him, but if I had listened, things would have gone better for me. Especially in my private life. I'm an expert at getting into unpleasant messes, and he was an expert counselor.

MARISTAIN: *How was his Catalan?*

PUIGDEVALL: Well, he read it perfectly well but he didn't speak it. His columns in the *Diari de Girona* were translated. That's pretty strange in itself. A writer who had won the Rómulo Gallegos Prize writing a column for a provincial newspaper. The *Diari de Girona* is great but Bolaño could have aspired to much more. One might deduce that perhaps he wasn't interested in the press. What's also interesting is the image of Gerona he portrayed in his literature. While many here write folklore, talking about the wonders of the scenery of the old quarter or the dry river that runs through the center of the city, the Gerona that one sees in Bolaño's literature is an unimportant town, like any other, a place that creates personal hells. Its only response is the same as that of all towns: nothing.

MARISTAIN: *What did you talk about, apart from your personal troubles?*

PUIGDEVALL: I remember spending a St. John's Eve with Enrique Vila-Matas, at the house they had rented in Blanes. Gonzalo

Herralde, Javier Cercas, and several more people were there, and I slept at his house in Blanes in Carrer del Lloro. When I woke up he was already writing. To rouse me from the landing strip in my head, he read some ancient Greek poetry to me, and over breakfast he explained what he'd be writing that morning. At lunchtime he told me what he'd be writing that afternoon, and when he came with me to the train station he told me what he'd be writing that night. It was a privilege because another of Bolaño's virtues is that he was an excellent storyteller in person. There are two ways to approach literature: one is dangerous and the other isn't. The safe way is to write it as it comes, without making it the central focus of your daily life. The other way is the opposite, and consists of converting everything that happens in your life into an opportune moment to write calmly or feverishly. Like Pere Gimferrer, a writer Bolaño admired very much, who was pure literature from his head to his toes. We don't see what's going on inside him. It would be just more literature.

MARISTAIN: *Is that your path?*

PUIGDEVALL: No, I'd like it to be now. I write because when I write, things don't happen to me and I don't get myself into trouble.

MARISTAIN: *What's your opinion of 2666?*

PUIGDEVALL: Well, it's a book that has the virtue of not being exhausted after a first reading. That would be impossible. It demands what all books demand out of pure selfishness: that you dedicate yourself to that book only. If someone were to start looking for all the hidden links, secrets, and mysteries in *2666*, they'd be working forever.

MARISTAIN: *You've witnessed the work of a writer who would become a leading light for a generation. What effect does that have on you?*

PUIGDEVALL: On the one hand, surprise and joy; on the other, sadness and annoyance, especially because of the myths that have sprung up around him. I'd have liked it much better if Bolaño had continued writing, even if he hadn't been so successful. All that adulation has nothing to do with literature.

MARISTAIN: *The fact that he had a street named after him makes you laugh . . .*

PUIGDEVALL: Yes, especially because it's a street on the outskirts of Gerona, in a lost suburb without buildings . . . That would have made Bolaño laugh.

MARISTAIN: *Where should one start to read Bolaño?*

PUIGDEVALL: I'd start with the stories so as to identify the recurring themes of his work. Then I'd go with his major works, *The Savage Detectives* and *2666*. And then his lesser but no less important ones, such as *By Night in Chile* and the rest . . .

MARISTAIN: *The recurring themes lead one to think about the value of themes in literature. In truth, Bolaño doesn't have many . . .*

PUIGDEVALL: Yes. The main one is literature. The characters are writers or people linked in some way to writing. There's violence, and there's sex. The women in his novels are very interesting. Love isn't one of his themes.

MARISTAIN: *Have you written anything influenced by Roberto's work?*

PUIGDEVALL: No. What I did do was address his cult, because Bolaño, one has to say, cultivated cults. I took a character he used a lot, the Belgian poet Sophie Podolski, and put her in one of my novels as a sort of homage to Bolaño.

MARISTAIN: *How do you feel when people ask you about Bolaño?*

PUIGDEVALL: I feel that everything has been said. At least everything that I could say. That we spoke a lot over the telephone, that we occasionally went out for dinner, and that he always ate my dessert if it was chocolate.

18

Mario Santiago and Trash Art

The diary of a compulsive writer—Books aren't his thing—The context justifies the text—The new tradition

The Spanish comedian José Mota says that he reads books in the shower so that he reads them only once. Long before him, Mario Santiago did something similar with books by Bolaño, as the writer complained in amusement during a television interview in Chile.

Few things are more certain about the life of Roberto Bolaño than the friendship and affection he felt for Mario Santiago Papasquiaro (1953–1998). He was born José Alfredo Zendejas Pineda, but called himself Mario so he wouldn't have the same name as José Alfredo Jiménez, the great Mexican singer, and added "Santiago Papasquiaro" as his surname to pay homage to the birthplace of the writer José Revueltas.

With a troubled history and a larger-than-life personality, beset by a serious addiction to alcohol from an early age, Mario Santiago died young in a traffic accident that his biographers describe as absurd. The poet embodied the revolutionary spirit that Bolaño desired throughout his life but couldn't or chose not to embrace in his adulthood. Indeed, Santiago took the stance of the *maudit* poet to the extreme and paid for it with his life— a fantasy Bolaño surely had for himself.

In the 1970s, Santiago was a scary person who was difficult to follow, a work of poetry in himself.

Carla Rippey says that in Mario Santiago's final years, it was difficult to let him into her house because "he never left." The writer Carmen Boullosa identifies him as the one she feared the most.

Ramón Méndez, his comrade at the founding of Infrarealism,

describes him as being much "more intelligent, astute, and cultured" than Bolaño. Juan Pascoe, José María Espinasa, and José Vicente Anaya all continued to see him occasionally after Bolaño left for Spain, and they generally agree on describing him as a unique character who lived a tragic life, a man who was committed to a bohemian lifestyle and writing unorthodox poems in notebooks, loose pages, and on walls.

As Luis Felipe Fabre wrote in *Letras Libres*, Mario Santiago was "a cult author for a few initiates, he wrote more than two thousand poems in the margins of other people's books, on napkins and other pieces of scrap paper, although he published only one book in his life, *Aullido de cisne* (The Howl of the Swan, 1996), and a small pamphlet titled *Beso eterno* (Eternal Kiss, 1995), neither of which had a large circulation."[1]

Santiago's widow, Rebeca López García, remembers: "He wrote every day, all the time. Even if he hadn't picked up a pen he was processing everything poetically. All the experiences were interwoven with what he was reading, with films and paintings.[2]

"He walked all day and he wrote as he went, on whatever he had at hand: a newspaper, or the book he was reading at the time," she recalls. "He stopped, wrote, continued walking ... he wrote on a metro ticket or a napkin."[3]

In 2006, the Fondo de Cultura Económica published *Jeta de santo* (A Saintly Face), an anthology of Santiago's poetry edited by his wife and his friend Mario Raúl Guzmán. This was a project supported by Roberto Bolaño, who offered it to the publisher Acantilado, but he died before he could put the idea into action. It was Juan Villoro and Alejandro Aura[4] who finally brought about the publication of the anthology.

According to the researcher, poet, and writer Luis Felipe Fabre,[5] the compiler and writer of the prologue to *Arte y basura: Una antología poética de Mario Santiago Papasquiaro* (Art and Trash: An Anthology of the Poetry of Mario Santiago Pa-pasquiaro)[6]: "Mario Santiago Papasquiaro was Mario Santiago Papasquiaro's best work. His real name was José Alfredo Zende-jas, and the invention of the new name was part of a new literary construct. He created a character for himself."

To Fabre, Mario's poetry is "self-referential, especially to the character he created himself." When his supporters got upset, insisting that Mario Santiago was a real person and not just a character created by Roberto Bolaño for *The Savage Detectives* (Ulises Lima), Fabre's reaction was "I don't think that he'd mind that at all. Mario himself started to create elements of the legend right from the beginning.

"I think that Ulises Lima is Mario Santiago and he isn't," said Fabre, who discovered the poet after reading *The Savage Detectives*, "because that's what happens with Roberto's novel: he makes a reference to his life or anything else, and we readers become detectives."

Fabre considers *The Savage Detectives* to be "fundamental" to the novel genre. "The novel provides the context for an impos-sible text. Bolaño never gives you the poem, but he provides the context in which it was created," he says.

Aiming to discover the life force, the roots of the work, Fabre found it difficult to gain access to Mario Santiago's unpublished writings. He overcame this disappointment by going through thousands of texts and papers.

FABRE: I was afraid of finding the work and killing it, letting it die inside me. Of starting to read his poems and saying: "Well, there's nothing here." I don't like Bolaño's poetry, and I think that his failure in the genre is made up for by his ability to tell the story in the narrative. In finding the potential poems of Mario Santiago, the idea of the absent poem, the impossible poem, was useful to me. At first there is a kind of disappointment: there are good things but he's not a great poet by my definition of the term. He's not Fernando Pessoa or Rimbaud when you get down to it. I suddenly realized that it really is an impossible work. One can only approach the work partially. Because there's so much of it, and so much of it is trash, you can't publish everything. So Bruno Montané said to me from Spain: "Here is the selection of poems by Mario Santiago that we were thinking of publishing." Essentially, he was a compulsive writer. He wrote all the time on whatever surface was available.

My theory is that even the books he published in his lifetime were anthologies. He gathered poems together, but he wasn't an author of books. I don't think books were his thing. Another problem is that literary criticism isn't as modern or advanced as art criticism. We're a lot further behind and don't read the context of written work. We're still tied to the text as the only form—and the fact is that Mario Santiago *was* his texts, but they were also part of him as performance. If you read a poem by Mario Santiago you might be disappointed, but if I were to tell you that it is written on the margins of a poem by Alfonso Reyes, now it becomes apparent that it is an intervention, to use a term from art criticism. You're not looking at a finished work, but a work continually being written, almost a work in process.

I don't think that Mexican poetry is classical but classist. It's interesting to me, then, that Mario Santiago existed: confronted with the perfect, pure, polished poets of the Mexican establishment, he in some way rejected the masterpiece.

This is my interview with Luis Felipe Fabre.

MARISTAIN: *How did you meet Mario Santiago's children?*

FABRE: I met them through Juan Villoro. At first I tried to find them through the post-Infra poets, Ramón Méndez and others. They're angry with Roberto Bolaño and they'll certainly be very annoyed with the anthology we're going to publish, mainly because they're not the ones bringing it out. When *Jeta de santo* came out, they were angry too, because the book was published by the Fondo de Cultura Económica. They felt that their saint was being taken away from them. They have this jealous, envious attitude to anything related to Mario and not them. It annoys them.

MARISTAIN: *I suppose that Mario's children aren't very involved with the arguments about the figure of their father . . .*

FABRE: Well, I think that they're scared. They're orphaned children, after all. They're adults but still alone in the world. A boy and a girl who live well in the apartment they inherited from their mother, who seems to have been a very well-organized and responsible woman. They love their father, which makes me think that in spite of all the chaos, in spite of all the difficulties that come with having an alcoholic in the family whom you have to drag home from the street and who eventually dies in a traffic accident, Mario was a good dad. He was called Mowgli like the character from *The Jungle Book*, and the girl was called Nadja like the text by André Breton. The children have a shrine to their father, with photos and things that he liked. They have been very generous to me, even though they grew up listening to their father's friends badmouthing the "literary establishment." In reality you can't build an establishment around a poet. If you write poetry you're already on the margins. They've kept their father's library almost untouched, and every time one of these "friends" comes they steal something from it. They complain about Mexican poets but then steal books with texts written by Mario Santiago.

MARISTAIN: *Do Mario Santiago's children talk about Bolaño?*

FABRE: Not much. I don't think that he's an easy figure for them either, especially because of what they've heard people say about him. I think that it's Bolaño's offensive success, that he became everything they aren't, that made them so upset with him. Also, I think that Roberto was a better friend to Mario than Mario was to him; one must also acknowledge that Mario couldn't handle himself properly. But I found some interesting things, such as an unpublished poem dedicated to Bolaño that addresses Infrarealism. It's one of the best in the book that we're putting together. I also think that to Roberto Bolaño, Mario Santiago represented the best of himself and he preferred to idealize him rather than have to deal with a friend in decline. Roberto infused him with the purity of youth, saying, "Here are my ideals." He gave Bolaño the image of the pure poet who doesn't sell out, the radical failure to which Mario committed himself. Bolaño was both scared and fascinated by it. "You took this further than I dared": I think there was something of that in their relationship.

MARISTAIN: *How do you think that Mario Santiago will be read by future generations?*

FABRE: Well, I think that in principle Mexico is a country that never had a literary avant-garde—at least I grew up thinking that. Suddenly, this man arrives from Chile, a country with a literary avant-garde par excellence, and he writes *The Savage Detectives* to prove the point that there was indeed an avant-garde in Mexico.

What Bolaño did changed how Mexican poetry of the 1970s was read, to some degree, and this is the context in which Mario Santiago should be seen. He's an important landmark in an alternative Mexican literary tradition. It used to be said that Mexican poetry lacked something of the street, and Mario Santiago is the quintessential voice of the street.

• • •

Marta Matas says that she doesn't understand what Roberto Bolaño liked about Blanes, a place she sees as "a town like any other, nothing special." Ponç Puigdevall goes further, mentioning the "bad taste" of living in the seaside town where *Mis últimas tardes con Teresa* (My Final Afternoons with Teresa), the famous novel by Juan Marsé, is set.

Nonetheless, Bolaño had become such a fixture in Blanes that when he started to get famous he was chosen to read the proclamation for the Fiestas Patronales in 1999, over which Juan Ramos Peña, the town's councillor, helped preside.

RAMOS PEÑA: I had the pleasure of meeting him in person in 1999. A few months before, I had been elected as a councillor for the municipality of Blanes by the Socialist Party of Catalonia. In the municipality it is a custom at the start of the Fiestas Patronales, held here in honor of Santa Ana, to ask a prominent figure from the world of culture or politics to give the proclamation for the fiestas. The full council—the mayor and all the councillors in the proper order—sits on a large dais in the central plaza, which is full of people. The proclaimer sits next to the mayor, who introduces them before the proclamation is read out. Once they've finished, the mayor introduces the full council to the proclaimer and then they all go off for a meal in a restaurant in the town. That year, we ate with Roberto Bolaño at the restaurant at the Horitzó Hotel in Blanes.

Today, Blanes is famous for more than being the setting of Marsé's novel but also because Bolaño lived there. Bolaño had his apartment on Rambla Joaquim Ruyra, close to the house that Carolina López shared with their children. The accessories store where he worked at one time, once owned by his mother, was at Carrer Colom 28. The Blanes library has a Roberto Bolaño room, whose door bears a plaque with the phrase: "I only hope to be considered a more or less decent South American writer who lived in Blanes and loved this town."

Bolaño has become part of the illustrious heritage of the city. After his death, Blanes has seen plenty of fans come and go in search of traces of the author. Many go to Narcís Serrs's video store, which Bolaño mentioned in his "Blanes Proclamation." Bolaño fondly recalled Serrs, who he said had one of the best senses of humor in town. He would spend whole afternoons talking about Woody Allen films or cult thrillers that few knew about.

"He started to come to my store in the nineties, more or less. He was interested in every film genre and we had good times talking about films," Serrs says. "He liked the cult English director Alex Cox, who directed the 1984 film *Repo Man*, a lot. We also spoke about other things, religion, politics, culture in general.

"I remember him as a simple person, who always wore a long coat, had a newspaper under his arm and a couple of books in his hands. What I most like about him when I remember him is that he was always the same person before and after he was famous," he recalls.

SERRS: He was a friend. We often went for a coffee together. At first he was a little brusque: he came into the store declaring that he was a writer and a poet and no one knew it. He used to say that either he'd live from literature or he wouldn't live. The last time I saw him, he was in a bar with a lot of people and he called me over. We spoke for a good while. When I left the bar, some people stopped me to ask if that was Roberto Bolaño. He was already very famous in Blanes.

I found out about his death from the television and went to the funeral in Barcelona, but I couldn't go to see him at the hospital. It was very quick; there wasn't time.

"Roberto and I were close friends, he came to my house every day and his death was a great loss," says the local baker Joan Planells, who arranged for the Blanes library to have a room named after Bolaño. "He was a great father, an excellent husband, and one of the best friends I've ever had. To me he was a wise man: he knew everything, he was a bottomless fount of knowledge. He knew about literature, painting, cinema, everything," he remembers.

"He came into the pastry shop to get pastries that didn't have sugar for his son and used to joke about his disease," Planells continues. "I found out about his death when I was in Sweden. It was on the first page of the newspaper *El País*. It was a shock, especially because before I left for northern Europe he said to me, 'Come back soon, I don't have much time left.' I told him not to joke about things like that, but now I know that he wasn't joking. He wasn't changed by the disease; he was always the same generous, good friend."

Bolaño's disease, as the liver specialist Victor García Blasco, to whom *The Insufferable Gaucho* is dedicated—Bolaño was more of a friend than a patient and they used to discuss literature—

confirmed to the Chilean magazine *Qué Pasa*, wasn't related to alcohol, and certainly not heroin, which he never took. It was a disease of the immune system.

"He had an immune disorder that affects the bile ducts and damages the liver," said the doctor. "It is a slow-acting disease. At first he was more worried than anything, and he was fine for a long while. But he suffered the torment of being sick: he was very sensitive and any test or exploratory procedure was anguish to him."

"I was poor, I lived on the streets and I thought of myself as a lucky guy because in the end I didn't catch anything serious," says the Blanes baker Planells. "I had a lot of sex, but I never caught a venereal disease. I read a lot, but I never wanted to be a successful author. Even losing my teeth was a kind of homage to Gary Snyder, whose life as a Zen wanderer meant that he didn't take care of his teeth. But everything comes."

And everything came.

Notes

Introduction

1. See full quote on p. 67.

Chapter 1: When His Father Bought Him a Horse

1. See interview with Eliseo Álvarez in *Turia*, Barcelona, June 2015. In English translation, the interview is "Positions Are Positions and Sex Is Sex," *Roberto Bolaño: The Last Interview and Other Conversations*, p. 75.
2. Roberto Bolaño to the Argentine journalist Demián Orosz, in an interview for *La voz del interior* newspaper, published on December 26, 2001.
3. This interview with León Bolaño was recorded by the Chilean documentarian Ricardo House, and is taken from his film with Ignacio Echevarría, *Roberto Bolaño, la batalla futura* (The Future Battle), a documentary in three parts.
4. León Bolaño, in a 2010 interview with the journalist César Tejeda for the magazine *Los suicidas*.

Chapter 2: Mama's Asthma

1. León Bolaño, in a 2010 interview with the journalist César Tejeda for the magazine *Los suicidas*.
2. See Jaime Quezada, *Bolaño Antes de Bolaño: Diario de Una Residencia en México, 1971–1972*, Chile: Catalonia, 2007.
3. See my interview with Carmen Boullosa, pp. 53–54.

4. See Andrés Gómez Bravo's interview "Mi hijo no se dejaba dominar por nadie" in *La Tercera Cultura*, October 7, 2006.
5. This quote comes from my interview with Juan Pascoe. See interview starting on p. 31.

Chapter 3: Mr. Beach's Son

1. León Bolaño, in a 2010 interview with the journalist César Tejeda for the magazine *Los suicidas*.
2. The story is part of a collection of thirteen, published as *Putas Asesinas* in 2001 ("Last Evenings on Earth" is published as part of an eponymous collection in English). In the story in question, the significant autobiographical aspects, confirmed by the writer's father, reflect the strange nature of the relationship between the two very different people, with the son seeming confused and bewildered by his father's presence.
3. Jaime Quezada, in *Bolaño antes de Bolaño* (Bolaño Before Bolaño).
4. In an interview with Ricardo House for the documentary *Roberto Bolaño, la batalla futura*.
5. Victoria Soto's account is contradicted by Roberto's stepmother, Irene, who went to live with the writer in Guadalupe Tepeyac for two years.

Chapter 5: The Origins of the Infrarealists

1. Roberto Bolaño interviewed on the Chilean television program *Off the Record*.
2. José Cristian Páez in *El Mercurio*.
3. Bolaño bought *Obra gruesa* in a bookshop in Santiago de Chile when he went back in 1973 at age twenty, after an extremely long journey over land and sea from Mexico. He also got hold of a copy of *Las musiquillas de las pobres esferas* (Tunes from Poor Areas) by Enrique Lihn and a book by Jorge Tellier. Montané and Bolaño met again in exile in Spain. In Barcelona, they published the magazine *Berthe Trépat*, named after one of the characters, the pianist, from *Hopscotch* by Julio Cortázar. They also published some poems by Enrique Lihn, with whom Roberto kept up a correspondence. According to Bolaño: "I met Lihn when I was having a bad, very bad time in Gerona. I lived in a very large house in the country with my dog. The dog and I were about to become a pair of hermits, complete savages. I think that people were

even scared to go to the house. Not because of the dog: because of me. And I thought that my relationship with literature was over. It's not that I stopped writing, but the flow of literature, seeing one's literature in the context of that of other people, was over. Then I suddenly started a wonderful correspondence with Enrique Lihn. He read my poems in Chile, but mostly it was that he listened to me and wrote back. He dug me out of the hole I was in pretty quickly."

4. Roberto Bolaño interview, *Off the Record*.

5. "Something amazing happened to us at the time. Someone painted a graffiti slogan that read: 'SEND BOLAÑO BACK TO SANTIAGO; SANTIAGO TOO.' They were sending him to Chile, somewhere he'd never been. The slogan was so good that I sometimes thought that Mario had done it himself and attributed it to our enemies. It was very funny." From an interview with María Teresa Cárdenas and Erwin Díaz, for *El Mercurio* of Chile.

6. Roberto Bolaño interview, *Off the Record*.

7. From an interview with María Teresa Cárdenas and Erwin Díaz for *El Mercurio* of Chile.

8. See Roberto Bolaño, "First Infrarealist Manifesto." An English translation by Tim Pilcher, which is quoted here, is available at launiversidad-desconocida.wordpress.com/2010/05/12/first-infrarealist-manifesto-2/.

9. José Ramón Méndez Estrada says that "three wanderers already in the realm of travelers who can never return" are Mario Santiago Papasquiaro, 1953–1998; Roberto Bolaño, 1953–2003; and Cuauhtémoc Méndez, 1956–2004. The latter is portrayed as Moctezuma Rodríguez in *The Savage Detectives*.

10. Coffee was another of the young writer's weaknesses: "He'd tell me to leave a kettle on the stove because he always drank coffee." Roberto was in the habit of writing at night. "He'd often see something in the street and start to write as soon as he got back," accompanied by cigarette smoke, the taste of coffee, and occasionally a glass of red wine, said Roberto's stepmother, María Irene Mendoza, to Magda Díaz y Morales for *aQROpolis*, the cultural supplement of *Plaza de Armas Querétaro, El Periódico de Querétaro*.

11. "Almost two years after the revolt of 1974 in the poetry workshop run by the Cultural Promotion department of the Universidad Nacional Autónoma de México (UNAM), when a group of rebel poets called for the resignation of its then coordinator Juan Bañuelos, the Infrarealist

movement was started between the end of 1975 and the start of 1976, in a building on Calle Argentina in the Historic Center of Mexico City, where Bruno Montané lived. The idea for the name and the foundation of a movement against official culture came from Roberto Bolaño, who was enthused by the irreverent poetry of a few young men. We continued to see each other after we were thrown out of the Bañuelos workshop." Ramón Mendez in the newspaper *La Jornada* of Morelos in 2004.

12. The interview with Ramón Méndez was carried out by Ricardo House for the documentary *Roberto Bolaño, la batalla futura*.

13. The supplement was edited by the poet Efraín Huerta, whom Bolaño considered as close a friend as Mario Santiago.

14. José María Espinasa was born in Mexico City on October 15, 1957. He is a writer and poet, the director of Ediciones Sin Nombre and coordinator of editorial production at the Colegio de México. He writes for *Casa del Tiempo, Intolerancia, La Jornada Semanal, La Orquesta, Nitrato de Plata, Novedades, Nueva Época, Tierra Adentro,* and *Vuelta.*

15. The interview with José María Espinasa was carried out by Ricardo House for *Roberto Bolaño, la batalla futura*.

16. "The first edition of *El Zaguán* [1975–1977] came out at the start of 1976. From the beginning the group of young poets revealed that they had confused the type of poetry that they liked with poetry in general. They took on a conservative theoretical and formal position (contemporary and *surrealizing*) that was no longer relevant. These young orthodox poets decided to imitate their elders and as if that wasn't enough, also gave them the best pages in their magazine. A final audit of the seven editions doesn't favor the young poet-editors. Next to the creations of the new, young, improvised academy was output and poems from some of their mentor figures and others that, if they didn't deserve the moniker, at least had the ambiguous sheen of prestige: Octavio Paz, Ramón Xirau, Concha Méndez, Jorge Guillén, José Emilio Pacheco, Álvaro Mutis, Pedro Garfias, Ernesto Mejía Sánchez, José de la Colina, Juan García Ponce, José Gorostiza, Manuel Durán, Jaime Sabines, Rubén Bonifaz Nuño, Aurelio Arturo, Vicente Alexandre, Salvador Elizondo, Tomás Segovia, Juan Gustavo Cobo Borda, Ulalume González de León, Rivanildo da Silva, and Luis Cardoza y Aragón." *Nexos* magazine, February 1, 1978.

17. Ediciones Asunción Sanchís, México–Lora del Río, 1976; introduction

by Juan Cervera; authors: José Vicente Anaya, Mara Larrosa, Cuauhtémoc Méndez, Bruno Montané, Rubén Medina, José Peguero, Mario
Santiago, and Roberto Bolaño.

18. *Muchachos desnudos bajo el arcoíris de fuego*, Editorial Extemporáneos,
Mexico, 1979; anthology edited by Roberto Bolaño; authors: Luis
Suardíaz, Hernán Lavín Cerda, Jorge Pimentel, Orlando Guillén,
Beltrán Morales, Fernando Nieto Cadena, Julián Gómez, Enrique
Verástegui, Roberto Bolaño, Mario Santiago, and Bruno Montané.
Prologue by Miguel Donoso Pareja. Dedication: "A las muchachas
desnudas bajo el arcoíris de fuego" (To the naked girls under the rain-
bow of fire). Preliminary warning: "Este libro debe leerse de frente y
de perfil, que los lectores parezcan platillos voladores"

19. *What do you think is Pablo Neruda's best poem?* "Almost any in *Residencia
en la Tierra*," Roberto Bolaño in an interview with Mónica Maristain
published in *La última entrevista a Roberto Bolaño y otras charlas con
grandes autores* (*Roberto Bolaño: The Last Interview and Other Conversations*), Editorial Axial, 2010.

20. Enrique "Poli" Délano is a major Chilean author who was born in
Madrid in 1936. The nickname Poli was given to him by Pablo Neruda
when he was a newborn baby to describe his large size and weight:
"That boy is Polyphemus."

21. Rodrigo Quijada in an interview with Ricardo House for *Roberto
Bolaño, la batalla futura*.

Chapter 6: Scribblers

1. October 20, 2009.

2. The jury for the eleventh Rómulo Gallegos International Prize for the
Novel was made up of Saúl Sosnowski (Argentina), Antonio Benítez
Rojo (Cuba), Ángeles Mastretta (Mexico), Hugo Achugar (Uruguay),
and Carlos Noguera (Venezuela). They met in Caracas to judge 220
novels from nineteen different countries. The jury unanimously short-
listed ten novels: *Las nubes* by Juan José Saer (Argentina), *La tierra
del fuego* by Sylvia Iparraguirre (Argentina), *Los detectives salvajes* by
Roberto Bolaño (Chile), *Caracol Beach* by Eliseo Alberto (Cuba),
Dime algo sobre Cuba by Jesús Díaz (Cuba), *Mariel* by José Prats Sa-
riol (Cuba), *Plenilunio* by Antonio Muñoz Molina (Spain), *Inventar
ciudades* by María Luisa Puga (Mexico), *Margarita, està linda la mar*
by Sergio Ramírez (Nicaragua), and *Historias de la marcha a pie* by

Victoria de Stefano (Venezuela). Eventually, by a majority of four votes, the winner was announced as *The Savage Detectives* by Roberto Bolaño. The award ceremony was held on August 2, 1999, in the presence of Chancellor of the Republic José Vicente Rangel and Minister of Interior Relations Ignacio Arcaya.

3. From Bolaño's article "On Literature, The National Literature Prize, and the Rare Consolations of the Writing Life," p. 110.

4. Interview with Mónica Maristain for the Argentine newspaper *Pagina/12*.

5. The publisher that previously promoted the boom authors.

6. From the article "Fragments of a Return to the Native Land," published by Bolaño in the Chilean magazine *Paula* and reproduced by Ignacio Echevarría in *Between Parentheses*, translated by Natasha Wimmer, pp. 61–74.

7. From the article "The Corridor with No Apparent Way Out," published by Bolaño in the now defunct magazine *Ajo Blanco* and part of *Between Parentheses*, translated by Natasha Wimmer, pp. 75–83.

8. Taken from Gabrielli's blog at www.letralia.com.

Chapter 7: Two Dissidents and a Lonely Gaucho

1. In 2013, Anagrama published another Piglia novel, *El camino de ida* (The Journey Out).

2. *The Insufferable Gaucho*, New Directions, 2010, translated by Chris Andrews, p. 28.

3. See *Between Parentheses*, translated by Natasha Wimmer, pp. 19–27.

Chapter 8: A Real Son of Parra

1. See "Eight Seconds with Nicanor Para," which was originally for the exhibit *Visual Artifacts: Address Required*. In English, see *Between Parentheses*, translated by Natasha Wimmer, p. 375.

2. Article published by Bolaño in the Chilean magazine *Paula* under the title "Fragments of a Return to the Native Land," which Ignacio Echevarría later included in *Between Parentheses*.

3. Interview with Carolina Roja published in the Argentine newspaper *Clarín*, April 4, 2012.

4. Ibid.

5. Interview with Juan Pablo Abalo and Paz Balmaceda.

Chapter 9: Roberto Did Very Strange Things

1. Bolaño to the Chilean television program *Off the Record*.

Chapter 11: The False Executor

1. With this journalist, during the recording of an interview for the documentary *Roberto Bolaño, la batalla futura*, by Ricardo House.
2. A Spanish writer born in 1960, author of *El tiempo de las mujeres* (The Time of Women), *Enterrar a los muertos* (Burying the Dead) *and La ternura del dragón* (The Dragon's Tenderness), among others.
3. For "Sevilla Kills Me" and "The Vagaries of the Literature of Doom," see *Between Parentheses*. "The Myths of Cthulhu" was originally prepared for the First Conference of Latin American Writers, June 2003, but Bolaño instead delivered the talk "Sevilla Kills Me," which was first collected in *Palabra de América* (Barcelona: Seix Barral, 2003, pp. 17–21), which collects twelve of the presentations from the June 2003 conference. "The Myths of Cthulhu" is collected in *The Insufferable Gaucho*.

Chapter 12: When Bolaño Murdered a Skinhead

1. From Bolaño's last interview: "Who are your closest friends?" "My best friend was the poet Mario Santiago, who died in 1998. Currently three of my best friends are Ignacio Echevarría, Rodrigo Fresán, and A. G. Porta."
2. Dante's *Inferno* (1935), starring Spencer Tracy, Rita Hayworth, and Claire Trevor.

Chapter 13: "These days it's very easy to say that you were a friend of Bolaño's"

1. Jorge Volpi, "Bolaño, Epidemia" (Bolaño Epidemic), published in several magazines, including the University of Mexico's journal in 2003. It is also the final essay in *Mentiras contagiosas* (Contagious Lies).
2. Volpi was a cultural attaché in Paris during the government of Vicente Fox between 2000 and 2006.
3. An Argentine writer born in 1974.
4. A French literary critic living in Mexico. He was a finalist in the

Anagrama Prize for nonfiction for his book *The Savage Writers*, which included Bolaño.

5. Álvaro Matus, "Dos valientes a la deriva" (Two Brave Men on a Wander), in *La Nación*, Buenos Aires, March 26, 2006.

6. Interview with Irene, León Bolaño's second wife, by Magda Díaz y Morales for *aQROpolis*, cultural supplement of the *Plaza de Armas Querétaro, El Periódico de Querétaro*, October 2011.

7. *Writing*, Lumen Editions, 1998.

8. The text was published in *Between Parentheses*, translated by Natasha Wimmer, p. 339.

9. Bolaño read "Los mitos de Cthulhú," which appeared in the magazine *Lateral* and then in *The Insufferable Gaucho*, New Directions.

Chapter 14: Pretty Stubborn with Women

1. Sergio González Rodríguez appears as a character in *2666*, "which I consider an honor because the novel very much impressed me. It is very difficult to describe the sensation of seeing yourself in a literary work and such a dramatic setting even though it was something that happened to me. Only when it is re-created by a masterful writer like Roberto Bolaño can one really understand the dimension of that human drama." *El Informador*, September 2010.

2. For more on the relationship between Bolaño and Sergio González Rodríguez, see Marcela Valdes, "Alone Among the Ghosts," *The Nation*, December 8, 2008.

3. The novel by Javier Marías is *The Dark Back of Time*, Alfaguara, 1998.

4. The interview with Paloma Díaz was carried out by Ricardo House for *Roberto Bolaño, la batalla futura.*

5. "She married Ermilo Abreu Gómez, with whom she had a difficult relationship, and gave birth to Juana Inés (1939). She divorced him when he belittled her maternal responsibilities. Her daughter married Bernardo Díaz, 'Porfirio Díaz's great-grandson,' and she kept their secret, much to the anger of Ermilo Abreu Gómez. Ninfa moved to Mexico, at first to her aunt Lupe's house, but she left there because of the strictures imposed upon her by her aunt. In 1953, she worked as an assistant in the Mexican delegation to the Organization of American States. There, she began her diplomatic career. In 1958, she was appointed vice-consul. In 1963, she went to New York. In 1967, she went to Rome

(Italy), where she lived for thirteen years. She eventually returned to Mexico, where she died on July 26, 1990." From an article written in 2008 by the Costa Rican Miguel Fajardo Korea.

6. From a letter to Paloma Díaz from Gerona.

7. Carla Rippey's ex-husband is the Mexican politician Ricardo Pascoe, one of the founders of the left-wing PRD party, which he left in 2003. He later became ambassador to Cuba for the government of Vicente Fox (2000–2006). Ricardo introduced Roberto to Juan Pascoe, his first publisher.

8. María and Angélica Font in the novel.

9. Interview with Andrés Gómez Bravo for *La Tercera*, Chile, October 2006.

10. "He took lots and lots and lots of care of me," said Lautaro Bolaño to Erik Haasnoot for the documentary *Bolaño cercano* (Intimate Bolaño). The interview with Marta Matas was held on the terrace of a bar in Blanes, on the beachfront. As she was saying how important Lautaro had been to his father, the boy passed by. He stopped and had a friendly conversation with the recording crew.

11. Andrés Gómez Bravo in *La Tercera*, Chile, in 2006.

12. Two English sources that mention the separation are Marcela Valdes, "Alone Among the Ghosts," *The Nation*, December 8, 2008, and Larry Rohter, "A Chilean Writer's Fictions Might Include His Own Colorful Past," *New York Times*, January 27, 2009.

13. For the documentary *Bolaño cercano*.

Chapter 15: Final Days

1. Dés wrote: "I feel like one of your characters: lost, defeated, and without having drawn any worthwhile conclusions."

2. Jesús Ferrero, a Spanish writer born in 1952, wrote in his blog: "One afternoon in Pamplona, Roberto said to me: 'I'm writing a novel that's going to be called *Sounds of Sonora*. Do you like the title?' I said that I did, a lot. It sounded like noisy madness, losing oneself in the immensity of the desert. A poisonous, terrible madness. Rattlesnakes, smoking guns, Russian and Mexican roulette. Red dawns, starry nights that can overwhelm you with their mineral, devastating beauty. Stones. I suppose that he was referring to the novel that would eventually be called *The Savage Detectives*. Detectives burning with thirst, traveling through

Europe and Africa, that meet the fates of Rimbaud and Roussel. The tenacious, demented detectives in search of a vase-shaped woman: the primordial woman, the primordial lover, the one who saves your life in the desert and dies from the effort. One afternoon in Pamplona, Roberto said to me: 'I'm writing a novel that could kill me.' But he survived that novel and one more. I toast him on this winter night on which it genuinely hurts me that he is no longer around. And yet he will always be there."

3. The song composed by the deceased Antonio Vega for Nacha Pop is, extraordinarily—and certainly without Bolaño knowing it—another link to Mexico. When *Amores Perros*, the film by Alejandro González Iñárritu that transformed the last decade of Mexican cinema, came out in 1999, the song, which was written in 1987, was on the sound track. The film made Gael García Bernal an international star. It was Gael who was most often mentioned for the role of Arturo Belano in the frustrated attempt to film *The Savage Detectives*.

4. The joke is as follows: "A guy goes up to a girl in a bar and says: 'Hello, what's your name?' 'Nuria.' 'Nuria, do you want to fuck me?' Nuria answers: 'I thought you'd never ask.'"

Chapter 17: The Little Bolaños

1. Interview with Juan Pablo Villalobos by the author, for *Página/12* in Argentina.
2. Juan Pablo Villalobos in a text in Portuguese written for *Companhia das Letras* under the title "Gostamos tanto de Roberto Bolaño."
3. Pahuatlán, Puebla, Mexico, 1970. Author of the novels *Luz de luciérnagas* (The Light of Fireflies) and *Gotas de Mercurio* (Drops of Mercury), Montesinos.
4. Alejandro Zambra in *Homenatge a Roberto Bolaño, El Llop Ferotge art i poesia*, September 2008, special edition published by Jorge Morales, in Spanish and Catalan.
5. Bolaño called the heirs to José Donoso "the Donositos": "His followers, those who today carry Donoso's torch ... try to write like Graham Greene, like Hemingway, like Conrad, like Vonnegut, like Douglas Coupland, with varying degrees of success, with varying degrees of abjection, and through the lens of these bad translations they

undertake to read their master, to publicly interpret the great Chilean novelist." See *Between Parentheses*, translated by Natasha Wimmer, p. 109.

6. Bolaño's first novel, written with Antoni García Porta (A. G. Porta).

7. From the book *Bolaño antes de Bolaño* (Bolaño Before Bolaño), by Jaime Quezada, Editorial Catalonia.

8. "All I can say is that in Librería 22 I saw a guy come in for a newspaper and come out carrying the four volumes of *The Man Without Qualities* by Musil, just as I've seen [Felip] Ortega creating fans, willing to throw themselves under a bus for Gabriel Ferrater, Borges, or Ferlosio," wrote Javier Cervas in *El País*.

9. "I remember many things about Bolaño, because I very much liked him and, if I'm not wrong, the feeling was mutual. I remember the day that I met him, without knowing it was him, and also the last day I saw him, without knowing it would be the last. I remember telephone conversations that lasted hours and hours, literally. I remember the end of one of them, late into the night, when we had hung up because we were exhausted and our hands hurt from holding the telephone and he called me back up in shock to tell me that ETA had killed Ernest Lluch. I remember the afternoon when he told me, at his home, that he was sick, and I also remember that he didn't like talking about it with anyone except perhaps, I think, with my sister, who had a similar disease. I remember the shouts of joy over the telephone when he called me to say that *The Savage Detectives* had won the Rómulo Gallegos Prize. I remember that one night he called me excitedly to read the first review of *Soldiers of Salamis* to me over the phone. I remember all the people who made fun of his work, criticized it, or ignored it, and who now write about him as though they had been close friends. I remember an infinite amount more, but I especially remember his books. They're the only thing that really matters, because all of Bolaño is in them. The rest is literature and, needless to say, the bad kind." Javier Cercas in an interview with the magazine *Somos*, of *El Comercio* in Peru in 2006.

10. "I speak to fewer and fewer people about literature. It's very strange. I discussed it a lot with Roberto Bolaño. We'd go to eat and talk a lot about poetry. But Bolaño died." Jaume Vallcorba in an interview given to elmalpensante.com.

Chapter 18: Mario Santiago and Trash Art

1. Luis Felipe Fabre in *Letras Libres*, October 2008.
2. Rebeca López García (1966–2011), Mario Santiago's widow, in an interview with Alejandro Flores for his blog *The Enconomist*.
3. Ibid.
4. Alejandro Aura (1944–2008) was a poet and a Mexican cultural official, the ex-husband of the writer Carmen Boullosa and father of their two children, Maria and Juan.
5. Mexico City, 1974.
6. Editorial Almadía, 2012.

Index